Collins

Work on your
Grammar
Advanced **C1**

Collins

HarperCollins Publishers
77-85 Fulham Palace Road
Hammersmith
London W6 8JB

First edition 2013

Reprint 10 9 8 7 6 5 4 3 2 1 0

© HarperCollins Publishers 2013

ISBN 978-0-00-749967-0

Collins® is a registered trademark of HarperCollins Publishers Limited

www.collinselt.com

A catalogue record for this book is available from the British Library

Typeset in India by Aptara

Printed in Italy by LEGO SpA, Lavis, (Trento)

The material in this book has been written by a team from Language Testing 123, a UK-based consultancy that specializes in English language assessment and materials. The units are by Liz Gallivan and have been based on material from the Collins Corpus and the Collins COBUILD reference range.
www.languagetesting123.co

Contents

Introduction   **5**

    Is this the right book for me?   5

    What does this book contain?   5

    I'm a student: how can I use this book?   6

    Study tips   6

    I want to improve my grammar   6

    I'm a teacher: how can I use this book with my classes?   8

    Lesson plan   8

1 Adjectives (1)
Using prepositions to change the meanings of adjectives   **10**

2 Adjectives (2)
Using adjectives before and after nouns   **14**

3 Adjectives (3)
Forming adjectives from participles (adjective/noun/
adverb + *-ing* / *-ed* participle)   **18**

4 Adjectives and adverbs
Adjectives and adverbs with different forms and meanings   **24**

5 Possessive adjectives
Using possessive adjectives and pronouns before *-ing* participles   **28**

6 *those* + participle adjectives
Using *-ing* and *-ed* adjectives with *those*, and in relative clauses   **31**

7 Relative clauses
Whom and *which*   **34**

8 Conditionals
Using conditionals to express formality (conditional + *if* +
should | conditional + *if* + *were to* | inversion of conditionals)   **38**

9 Ways of using *as* and *though*   **41**

10 Using *it* as an object in sentences
it + adjective/noun + clause
it + person/institution + **to**-*infinitive*   **44**

11 Using comparative structures for cause and effect
The sooner, the better (*the* + a comparative adjective, adverb or
noun, *the* + a comparative adjective, adverb or noun or verb)   **47**

12 Using *-ing* clauses after certain verbs
verb + object + *-ing* clause   **50**

13 Focusing sentences (1)
Using *it* (*It's food that he wants*)   **54**

14 **Focusing sentences (2)**
Using *what* (*What you need is a doctor*) 57

15 **Using to-*infinitive* clauses as subject/object** 60

16 **Using negatives with reporting verbs**
think, expect, believe and *seem* 64

17 **Passives (1)**
Using passives when the active verb has two objects (*be + -ed* participle) 67

18 **Passives (2)**
Using passive *-ing* and *to* forms (*be + -ed* participle | *be + being + -ed* participle | *-ing* form + *-ed* participle) 72

19 **Future perfect**
Making predictions about the future (*will / should* + have + *-ed* participle | *will / should* + have been + *-ing* participle) 75

20 ***Should* and the subjunctive**
Using reported clauses with and without modals 78

21 **Avoiding repetition by omitting *to*-infinitives** 81

22 **Politeness**
Using past forms and *wonder* and *hope* to express politeness 85

23 **Sentence connectors and conjunctions** 88

24 ***Which, whose, how much* and *how many***
Asking questions about things outside the main clause 92

25 **Phrasal verbs (1)**
Two-word phrasal and prepositional verbs 96

26 **Phrasal verbs (2)**
Three-word phrasal and prepositional verbs 100

27 **Inversion (1)**
Inversion after *so* + adjective, *such* + be, *neither* and *nor* 103

28 **Inversion (2)**
Inversion after negative adverbials 106

29 **Inversion (3)**
Inversion after *as* and *than* 109

30 **Inversion (4)**
Inversion after adverbials of place 112

Answer key 115

Introduction

Welcome to *Work on your Grammar – Advanced (C1)*

Is this the right book for me?

This book, *Work on your Grammar – Advanced (C1)*, helps students to learn and practise English grammar at CEF level C1. This book is suitable for you to use if you are at CEF level C1, or just below.

So, what is CEF level C1? Well, there are six Common European Framework levels. They go up from A1 for beginners, A2, B1, B2, C1 and finally C2.

If the description below sounds like you, then this is probably the right book for you. If not, choose *Work on your Grammar – Upper Intermediate (B2)* (below this level).

- I can understand a wide range of texts and I can follow what almost everyone says, whether directly to me or on the TV and so on.

- I can express my feelings, opinions and ideas quite fluently.

- I can adjust to different situations in using English, for example from academic to work-based to social situations.

- When I write or speak, I can use a range of different grammatical structures and patterns.

- I'm aware that there are gaps in my knowledge and I make mistakes from time to time.

What does this book contain?

This book contains 30 units to help you learn and practise important grammar for this **Advanced (C1)** level.

Each unit explains the **grammar point** and then there is a series of **exercises** that gives you useful practice in this particular area. The exercises are there to help you really understand the grammar point and how to use it correctly. There are different types of exercise. This helps you to see different aspects of the grammar, and it means you have a range of practice to do.

The **answers** to all the exercises are at the back of the book.

Remember! boxes highlight important information about the grammar points, so it is a good idea to read them and think about them.

I'm a student: how can I use this book?

You can use this book in different ways. It depends on your needs, and the time that you have.

- If you have a teacher, he or she may give you some advice about using the book.

- If you are working alone, you may decide to study the complete book from beginning to end, starting with unit 1 and working your way through to the end.

- You might find that it is better to choose which units you need to study first, which might not be the first units in the book. Take control of what you learn and choose the units you feel are the most important for you.

- You may also decide to use the book for reference when you are not sure about a particular grammar point.

- You can find what you want to learn about by looking at the **Contents** page.

- Please note that, if you do not understand something in one unit, you may need to study a unit earlier in the book, which will give you more information.

Study tips

1 Read the aim and introduction to the unit carefully.

2 Read the explanation. Sometimes there is a short text or dialogue; sometimes there are tables of information; sometimes there are examples with notes. These are to help you understand the most important information about this grammar point.

3 Don't read the explanation too quickly: spend time trying to understand it as well as you can. If you don't understand, read it again more slowly.

4 Do the exercises. Don't do them too quickly: think carefully about the answers. If you don't feel sure, look at the explanation again. Write your answers in pencil, or, even better, on a separate piece of paper. (This means that you can do the exercises again later.)

5 Check your answers to the exercises using the **Answer key** at the back of the book.

6 If you get every answer correct, congratulations! Don't worry if you make some mistakes. Studying your mistakes is an important part of learning.

7 Look carefully at each mistake: can you now see why the correct answer is what it is?

8 Read the explanation again to help you understand.

9 Finally, if the unit includes a **Remember!** box, then try really hard to remember what it says. It contains a special piece of information about the grammar point.

10 Always return: come back and do the unit's exercises again a few days later. This helps you to keep the information in your head for longer.

I want to improve my grammar

Good! Only using one book won't be enough to really make your grammar improve. The most important thing is you!

Of course, you need to have a paper or electronic notebook. Try these six techniques for getting the best from it.

- *Make it real*: It's probably easier to remember examples than it is to remember rules. Often, it's better to try to learn the examples of the grammar, not the explanations themselves. For example, rather than memorizing 'You can use the present simple to talk about the future', you should learn 'My holiday starts on Monday'.

- *Make it personal*: When you're learning a new structure or function, try to write some examples about yourself or people or places you know. It's easier to remember sentences about your past than someone else's! For example, 'I'm studying art this year'.

- *Look out*: Everything you read or hear in English may contain some examples of the new grammar you're learning. Try to notice these examples. Also, try to write down some of these examples, so that you can learn them.

- *Everywhere you go*: Take your notebook with you. Use spare moments, such as when you're waiting for a friend to arrive. Read through your notes. Try to repeat things from memory. A few minutes here and there adds up to a useful learning system.

- *Take it further*: Don't just learn the examples in the book. Keep making your own examples, and learning those.

- *Don't stop*: It's really important to keep learning. If you don't keep practising, you won't remember for very long. Practise the new grammar today, tomorrow, the next day, a week later and a month later.

I'm a teacher: how can I use this book with my classes?

The content of this book has been very carefully selected by experts from Language Testing 123, using the Common European Framework for Reference, English Profile, the British Council Core Inventory, the Collins Corpus and material created for *Collins COBUILD English Grammar, Collins COBUILD Pocket English Grammar* and *Collins COBUILD English Usage*. As such, it represents a useful body of knowledge for students to acquire at this level. The language used is designed to be of effective general relevance and interest to any learner aged 14+.

The exercises use a range of types to engage with students and to usefully practise what they have learnt from the explanation pages. There are a lot of exercises in each unit so it is not necessary for students to do all the exercises at one sitting. Rather, you may wish to return in later sessions to complete the remaining exercises.

The book will be a valuable self-study resource for students studying on their own. You can also integrate it into your teaching.

The explanations and exercises, while designed for self-study, can be easily adapted by you to provide useful interactive work for your students in class.

You can use the units in the book to extend, back up or consolidate language work you are doing in class. The **Contents** will help you choose which units are most appropriate.

You may also find that you recommend certain units to students who are experiencing particular difficulty with specific language areas. Alternatively, you may use various units in the book as an aid to revision.

Lesson plan

1 Read the aim and introduction to the unit carefully: is it what you want your students to focus on? Make sure the students understand it.

2 Go through the explanation with your students. You may read it aloud to them, or ask them to read it silently to themselves. With a confident class, you could ask them to read some of it aloud.

3 If there is a dialogue, you could ask students to perform it. If there is a text, you could extend it in some way that makes it particularly relevant to your students. Certainly, you should provide a pronunciation model of focus language.

4 Take time over the explanation page, and check students' understanding using concept-checking questions. The questions will vary according to content, but they may be based on checking the time in verb tenses. For example, with the sentence, 'She came on the train that got here yesterday', you could ask, 'When did she arrive?'. This might elicit the correct answer 'yesterday' and the incorrect answer 'tomorrow', and you would know if your students understood the meaning of the past simple verb. Or you could ask, 'Where is she now?' and correct answers would include 'here' while incorrect answers would include 'on the train'.

5 Perhaps do the first exercise together with the class. Don't do it too quickly: encourage students to think carefully about the answers. If they don't feel sure, look together at the explanation again.

6 Now get students to do the other exercises. They can work alone, or perhaps in pairs, discussing the answers. This will involve useful speaking practice and also more careful consideration of the information. Tell students to write their answers in pencil, or, even

better, on a separate piece of paper. (This means that they can do the exercises again later.)

7 Check their answers to the exercises using the **Answer key** at the back of the book. Discuss the questions and problems they have.

8 If the unit includes a **Remember!** box, then tell students to try really hard to remember what it says. It contains a special piece of information about the grammar point.

9 Depending on your class and the time available, there are different ways you could extend the learning. If one of the exercises is in the form of an email, you could ask your students to write a reply to it. If the exercises are using spoken language, then you can ask students to practise these as bits of conversation. They can re-write the exercises with sentences that are about themselves and each other. Maybe pairs of students can write an exercise of their own together and these can be distributed around the class. Maybe they can write short stories or dialogues including the focus language and perform these to the class.

10 Discuss with the class what notes they should make about the language in the unit. Encourage them to make effective notes, perhaps demonstrating this on the board for them, and/or sharing different ideas from the class.

11 Always return: come back and repeat at least some of the unit's exercises again a few days later. This helps your students to keep the information in their heads for longer.

Adjectives (1)

Using prepositions to change the meanings of adjectives

In this unit you learn to use the right prepositions to change the meanings of the adjectives they follow.

Using the correct preposition

Some adjectives can be followed by a number of prepositions but the meaning changes depending on the choice of preposition. Look at the word **good** and six different prepositions that it can be followed by:

> *Do you know anyone who's **good at** mending bikes?*
> *Mum was really **good about** the broken vase. She didn't get upset with me.*
> *I should eat more fruit because I know it's **good for** me.*
> *I'm not **good with** crowds. They make me anxious.*
> *It was **good of** you to babysit last night. Thank you!*
> *I've been so **good to** you, and you give me nothing back.*

Here are some more adjectives that can be followed by different prepositions. Read the example sentences so that you can see the differences in meaning.

Adjective	Preposition	Example
accountable	for	I know what I'm doing and I'm **accountable for** my own choices!
	to	The administrative assistants are **accountable to** the head of the department.
afraid	of	Have you always been **afraid of** flying?
	for	I was really **afraid for** your safety. Sailing in a storm is dangerous!
bad	about	I feel really **bad about** forgetting Anna's birthday.
	at	I've always been **bad at** spelling.
	for	Everyone knows smoking is **bad for** your health
	with	I'm so **bad with** numbers. Maths has always been my weakest subject.
frightened	of	He's **frightened of** heights. That's why he'd never go mountain climbing.
	by	Horror movies don't usually bother me but I was really **frightened by** that film.
glad	of	It's great that I can give you a lift. I'll be **glad of** the company.
	about	He was really **glad about** his exam results.
	for	You won the competition! I'm so **glad for** you.
happy	at	She was **happy at** the idea of living in a new village.
	for	That's fantastic news! I'm so **happy for** you both.
	with	It took a long time to fix it, but he's very **happy with** the repair.
nice	about	I expected you to be far more angry with me. Thank you for being so **nice about** it.
	of	It was **nice of** him to take the time to talk to me.
	to	I like people who are **nice to** me.

responsible	for	Acid rain is **responsible for** considerable damage to the environment.
	to	The government is **responsible to** the National Assembly which has the power to force it out of office.
sorry	about	I'm really **sorry about** your mother's death.
	for	I do feel a bit **sorry for** her sometimes, although I'm sure she could make more of an effort.
upset	by	He was obviously quite **upset by** the remark.
	for	We were really **upset for** Pablo. What bad luck to get an injury just as he was establishing himself in the team!
	over	Martha got **upset over** something I said on Thursday evening.
	with	His supporters were **upset with** him for pulling out of the competition.

Exercise 1

Choose the correct word, as shown.

1 You looked so pale and drawn, my love. I felt so sorry **for** / **about** you!

2 Amy's a really good friend and I know I offended her. I don't feel very good **about** / **for** it.

3 You don't have to thank me. I was just glad **of** / **for** the chance to return a favour.

4 I thought I could trust Sebastian. I'm disappointed **in** / **at** him.

5 I just don't want Grace to get hurt. I'm afraid **of** / **for** her because she doesn't seem to realize the risk she's taking.

6 I can remember names but I'm really bad **for** / **at** remembering faces.

Exercise 2

Are the highlighted words correct or incorrect in this text?

Hi Gemma!

It was fun last night, wasn't it, even if it was a bit chilly in the garden? (We were really glad ¹**of** ☑ our sweaters!) It was really good ²**for** ☐ you to help out when Jamie got so upset ³**over** ☐ the dog last night – thank you so much! Poor Jamie has always been a bit anxious ⁴**around** ☐ dogs. I don't know why he's frightened ⁵**about** ☐ them. As far as I know, he's never had a bad experience with one. Is Joe OK this morning, btw? He looked so ill last night – I felt a bit sorry ⁶**for** ☐ him, standing out there in the cold.

Ooh, Jamie's calling – better go!

Love

Louisa

xxx

Exercise 3

Complete the sentences by writing one word in each gap, as shown.

| at | with | of | for | about | to |

1 It's really good _____ *of* _____ you to help us out at such short notice. We do appreciate it.

2 I know sugar's not good _____ me, but I'm kind of addicted to it.

3 My parents were really good _____ me when I was short of money. I'll never forget their generosity.

4 The thing is, I know I hurt her when I ended the relationship and I don't feel very good _____ that.

5 Tom, are you any good _____ sewing?

6 Ali's so good _____ children. It just comes naturally to him.

Exercise 4

For each sentence, tick the correct ending, as shown.

1 If something that you hoped would happen does not happen, you are
   ☐ disappointed in it.
   ☑ disappointed about it.

2 If you are kind to someone when they are unhappy or ill, you are
   ☐ good for them.
   ☐ good to them.

3 If something frightens you, you are
   ☐ afraid for it.
   ☐ afraid of it.

4 If you are grateful for having something, you are
   ☐ glad of it.
   ☐ glad for it.

5 If you can be blamed for something bad that has happened, you are
   ☐ responsible to it.
   ☐ responsible for it.

Exercise 5

Match the two parts, as shown.

1 We are responsible individuals and can be held accountable for

2 We were slightly disappointed at

3 Olga's always been terribly afraid of

4 Apparently, sitting all day is really bad for

5 Melissa would make a great teacher. She's so good at

6 We're so sorry about

a spiders.

b your dog having cancer.

c explaining complex concepts simply.

d the lack of facilities when we arrived at the campsite.

e the spine.

f all our actions.

Exercise 6

Are the highlighted words correct or incorrect in the sentences?

1 I felt responsible **for** ☑ all the offence that was caused.

2 Anyway, I've done all the work that needs to be done this week and I'm feeling really good **about** ❑ it.

3 Don't ask me to bake a cake. I'm really bad **with** ❑ cooking!

4 I'm so sorry **with** ❑ the noise we made last night. It was really thoughtless of us.

5 I thought Michael was a good friend. I'm afraid I'm a bit disappointed **in** ❑ him.

6 The Government is responsible **to** ❑ parliament.

Exercise 7

For each sentence, tick the correct ending.

1 Pedro has done a very small repair on my bike,
   ❑ but he's not very happy for it.
   ❑ but he's not very happy with it.
   ❑ but he's not very happy at it.

2 Maria has broken Paul's MP3 player
   ❑ and he's very upset about it.
   ❑ and he's very upset for it.
   ❑ and he's very upset with it.

3 My mother was very angry when she got home,
   ❑ and demanded to know who was responsible with the mess.
   ❑ and demanded to know who was responsible to the mess.
   ❑ and demanded to know who was responsible for the mess.

4 Felicity cannot seem to get a job
   ❑ and I feel really sorry for her.
   ❑ and I feel really sorry with her.
   ❑ and I feel really sorry about her.

5 When Jamil saw his friends after his father's death
   ❑ everyone was very nice of him.
   ❑ everyone was very nice to him.
   ❑ everyone was very nice about him.

Adjectives (2)

Using adjectives before and after nouns

In this unit you learn that some adjectives can only be used before a noun, while others are used after nouns.

Adjectives that do *not* come before nouns

When used with a particular meaning, some adjectives are normally used only *after* linking verbs like **be**. They are not used before nouns. You say *The boy was asleep*, NOT ~~an asleep boy~~, and you say *The plant was still alive*, NOT ~~an alive plant~~.

The following adjectives are normally used only *after* linking verbs.

alive	awake
hurt	ill
asleep	ready
alight	sorry
ashamed	sure
glad	well
alone	alike
afraid	

> *Remember!*
> Putting an adjective after a linking verb has the effect of focusing attention on the adjective.

Fortunately, there are other adjectives with similar meanings that you can use before the noun:

alive and **living**
   *I was the only **living** person in 100 miles.*

asleep and **sleeping**
   *The **sleeping** boy woke up when the door opened.*

hurt and **injured**
   *The **injured** animal ran away.*

alike and **similar**
   *I have a **similar** coat to that one.*

Other adjectives with similar meanings include:

afraid and **frightened**

alight and **burning**

alone and **solitary**

glad and **happy**

Adjectives with different meanings before or after the noun

There are a few adjectives that have a different meaning depending on whether they come before the noun or after it.

responsible

*A **responsible** person would take charge of the situation and sort it out!*
*The person **responsible** for this terrible thing should be punished.*

present

*The **present** students are not so hard working, unlike last year's group.*
*I'd like to say 'welcome' to all the students **present** at this meeting.*

concerned

*There are a lot of extremely **concerned** people who are worried about the damage that this will do.*
*Much to the relief of the families, the four people **concerned** were located.*

named

*The investigation found that the **named** individuals and firms colluded to decide who would win contracts.*
*The certificate is issued to the individual **named** below and must be returned before May 20.*

proper

*Why don't you enrol in the University and take a **proper** course?*
*Applicants may be required to complete a period of preliminary study before they are admitted to the diploma course **proper**.*

involved

*To choose between so many top-class designs has, inevitably, meant a very long and **involved** process.*
*With the help of demonstrators, you can see the process **involved** in producing a finished piece of jewellery.*

Adjectives that you can use after a noun

There are some adjectives that you can use after a noun when the noun has a superlative or **first, last, only, every** or **any** before it.

*Mrs Morgan is the **only teacher available** to take the class.*
*That's the **best result possible**!*
*I've got **every book written** on the subject.*
*He wrote the **most beautiful poetry imaginable**.*

Exercise 1

For each sentence, tick the correct ending.

1 She would never forget the
   ☐ afraid faces of the children as they clung to their parents.
   ☐ frightened faces of the children as they clung to their parents.

2 To her surprise, in the back of the car she saw
   ☐ two sleeping babies.
   ☐ two asleep babies.

3 The couples whose relationships endured were very compatible, with
   ☐ similar outlooks on life.
   ☐ alike outlooks on life.

4 In dramatic scenes last night, three men were rescued from the
   ☐ burning building.
   ☐ alight building.

5 In the distance, she spied
   ☐ a solitary figure.
   ☐ an alone figure.

Exercise 2

Are the highlighted words correct or incorrect in the sentences?

1 According to the poll, Rickman is the 19th greatest **living** ☐ film star.

2 With no **alive** ☐ relatives, and few surviving friends, Maggie is sometimes very lonely.

3 Paramedics arrived within minutes and took the **hurt** ☐ passengers to Queen Anne Hospital.

4 The **injured** ☐ soldiers were transferred to Rafah Central Hospital.

5 It was such a delight to see the children's **happy** ☐ faces.

6 So here's the question on every parent's lips: what does it take to raise **glad** ☐ children?

Exercise 3

Match the sentence halves.

1 Ever since the vaccine was approved more than a decade ago,

2 According to three of the people

3 No information about named individuals is given to third parties

4 The book outlines the history of the region from the seventeenth century

5 The Cup begins with two preliminary rounds

6 I wouldn't ever recommend anybody tackling a marathon

a without proper training.

b to the present day.

c before the first round proper involving the Premier League clubs.

d without written consent from the individuals concerned.

e present at the meeting, the biggest topic of conversation was staffing levels.

f concerned parents have been questioning its use.

Exercise 4

Which sentences are correct?

1 Pages 4 and 5 contain information about the involved people in the transatlantic slave trade. ☒

2 The putting together of classes is, as I'm sure you'll appreciate, a very involved process for our teachers. ☐

3 They were her parents and thus the ones responsible for her care and wellbeing. ☐

4 So are teenagers capable of being responsible parents? ☐

5 This morning we look at the origins of the present crisis in the region. ☐

6 If there are any present people when the officer arrives at the crime scene, he or she will detain them. ☐

Exercise 5

Match the two parts.

1 the present candidates

2 the candidates present

3 concerned patients

4 the patients concerned

5 an involved process

6 the process involved

7 the doctors responsible

8 responsible doctors

a patients affected by something

b doctors who can be trusted

c patients who are worried

d the doctors in charge of something or the doctors who did a particular thing

e a complicated process

f people who are candidates now

g candidates who are at an event

h the process that is a part of something

Exercise 6

Complete the sentences by writing one phrase in each gap.

| worst abuse | highest score | last man | first payment |
| only software | only thing |

1 Krystal was only five years old and had suffered some of the _____ imaginable for a child that age.

2 She got a total of 86, which is the _____ possible.

3 We resorted to burgers because it was the _____ available.

4 Seconds before impact, the _____ conscious in the cockpit of the doomed plane made a desperate call.

5 This advance payment shall be deducted from the _____ due, in accordance with paragraph 12.

6 The Vina package is the _____ in any way comparable with Jadd's.

Adjectives (3)

Forming adjectives from participles

adjective/noun/adverb + *-ing* / *-ed* participle

In this unit you learn to use adjectives formed from *-ing* and *-ed* participles, compound adjectives formed from noun/adjective/adverb + participle and also adjectives formed from preposition + participle.

| To: Helen |
| From: Sophie |
| Subject: Nick's boss |

Hiya Helen

Guess what? We had dinner last night with Nick's boss, Al, and his **long-suffering** wife. (I really don't know how she puts up with him!)

Al is one of the loudest, most opinionated people I've ever met, though not all bad. When you first meet him, his manner is quite **off-putting**, but you warm to him a bit as you get to know him. For one thing, he's very **thick-skinned** – you can say whatever you like to him and he's not **offended**.

Also, he's quite **easy-going**. Nick, (my **absent-minded** boyfriend!), had completely forgotten to buy a gift to take, so we arrived **empty-handed**, but Al was really nice about it.

Also, Nick hadn't warned me that he and Al would be wearing smart suits, so I did feel a little bit **underdressed** in my jeans!!

Oh, postman at the door – must dash.

Speak later

Love
Sophie

Adjectives formed from participles

Adjectives formed from the *-ed* participle

Most *-ed* adjectives have a passive meaning. They show that something has happened or is happening *to* the thing being described.

*She's a very **frightened** woman.*
*He had a **disappointed** expression on his face.*
*We have a long list of **satisfied** customers.*
*We cannot refuse to teach children the **required** subjects.*

A few **-ed** adjectives are related to intransitive verbs and have an active meaning.

> The **capsized** ship lay at the bottom of the ocean.
> She is the daughter of a **retired** army officer.
> Police are hunting three dangerous **escaped** prisoners.
> She was wearing **faded** jeans and a T-shirt.

Adjectives with the same form as irregular **-ed** participles that do not end in **-ed** are also known as **-ed** adjectives.

> Was it a **broken** bone or a **torn** ligament?
> He had a a black eye and a **swollen** mouth.
> The country road was blocked by a **fallen** tree.

Adjectives formed from the -ing participle

Some **-ing** adjectives describe the effect that something has on your feelings and ideas, or on the feelings and ideas of people in general. They can be used with words like **very** and **rather** and have comparatives and superlatives.

> There has been an **alarming** rise in accidents on this road.
> I had a **very amusing** evening.
> The whole experience is still **rather disturbing**.
> She spoke in a low voice that was far more **frightening** than a shout.
> He is the most **annoying** man I have ever met.

Other **-ing** adjectives are used to describe a process or state that continues over a period of time. They are **not** used with words like **very** and **rather** but can often be modified by adverbs that describe the speed with which the process happens.

> The rock band had a **fast-growing** number of fans.
> When I am driving in a car, I get very frustrated by **slow-moving** traffic.
> First time buyers are finding it difficult to keep up with **rapidly-rising** prices.

Adjectives formed from noun/adjective/adverb + participle

Compound adjectives are made up of two or more words.

These include:

adjective or adverb + **-ed** participle
> **low-paid**, **well-behaved**
> She went into her store, but came back **empty-handed**.
> I was in a **light-hearted** mood.
> A **well-balanced** diet includes all the necessary vitamins and supplements you are likely to need.

adjective, adverb or noun + **-ing** participle
> **good-looking**, **long-lasting**, **man-eating**
> There was no denying that Marta was quite a **nice-looking** girl.
> Their behaviour had made them feared in the community, not least by their **long-suffering** neighbour.
> He hung by one hand from his parachute strap in a **death-defying** stunt thousands of feet above the ground

noun + *-ed* participle

> *tongue-tied, wind-swept*
> He was breathing heavily and looked **panic-stricken**.
> The pictures are displayed in a **purpose-built** modern gallery.
> There was a row of **silver-plated** dishes on the hotplate.

Adjectives formed from preposition + participle

Some adjectives can be made from a preposition and a participle:

> *underdressed, overbearing, underachieving*
> Their gardens were **overgrown** with weeds and brambles.
> He looked **downcast** and nervous.
> The cake may be slightly **underdone** in the middle but it should be edible.
> He was trying to sound casual, but I could hear the **underlying** tension in his voice.
> The river was shadowed by **overhanging** branches.

> ### Remember!
>
> Compound adjectives are often written with a hyphen when they come before the noun, but without a hyphen when they come after the noun.

Exercise 1

Complete the sentences by writing one word in each gap.

| rising | anticipated | corrected | elected | empowering | insinuating |

1 I duly made the amendments and sent the _____ manuscript back to the publisher.

2 I gained a lot of confidence and self-worth from the course and generally found it to be an _____ experience.

3 So how will the bottled water industry respond to the _____ tide of criticism from environmentalists worldwide?

4 So, finally, here it is – the much _____ novel from the bestselling Swedish crime writer.

5 We must take steps to ensure that our _____ representatives reflect the profile of our members.

6 'You seemed quite friendly towards him yesterday,' she said, in an _____ tone that I took exception to.

Exercise 2

Rearrange the letters to find words, as shown. Use the definitions to help you.

1 fof-ttupnig ___*off-putting*___ (describes a quality or feature of something or someone that makes you dislike them, or not want to get involved with them)

2 banest-denimd _____ (describes a person who often forgets things or does not pay attention to what they are doing, often because they are thinking about something else)

3 bael-deidob _____ (physically strong and healthy; not disabled)

4 chitk-denkins _____ (not easily upset by criticism or unpleasantness)

5 ghilt-raedhet _____ (cheerful and happy)

6 nolg-solt _____ (describes someone or something that you have not seen for a long time)

Exercise 3

For each question, tick the correct answer.

1 If someone does not have a present to give a person that they are visiting, how might you describe them?
- ❑ empty-hand
- ❑ empty-handed
- ❑ empty-handing

2 If someone is unable to say anything because they feel shy or nervous, how might you describe them?
- ❑ tongue-tie
- ❑ tongue-tied
- ❑ tongue-tying

3 How would you describe an action that was extremely dangerous?
- ❑ death-defied
- ❑ death-defying
- ❑ death-defies

4 How would you describe someone who is so anxious or afraid that they may act without thinking carefully?
- ❑ panic-strike
- ❑ panic-stricken
- ❑ panic-stricking

5 How would you describe someone who patiently puts up with a lot of trouble or unhappiness, especially when it is caused by their husband or wife?
- ❑ long-suffer
- ❑ long-suffered
- ❑ long-suffering

Exercise 4

Complete each sentence with an adjective that combines 'over' or 'under' with a form of the verb in brackets.

1 I do think it's possible for a man to wear shorts without looking like an _____ (grow) schoolboy.

2 The school appointed a new member of staff responsible for helping _____ (achieve) children to realize their full potential.

3 I wouldn't go so far as to say he's a bad actor, but I certainly think he's _____ (rate).

4 The _____ (hang) branches of my neighbour's trees mean that my garden is in almost perpetual shadow.

5 If we are to solve the problem of poverty we must first identify the _____ (lie) causes.

6 Three waiters had called in sick that evening, so the restaurant was seriously _____ (staff).

Exercise 5

Decide if the pairs of sentences have the same meaning, as shown.

1 **A** I met Sean and his long-suffering wife.
  B I met Sean and his wife, who suffers from a chronic illness. ✘

2 **A** Lucy is very insensitive, and very thick-skinned.
  B Lucy is very insensitive, and she doesn't mind if you criticize her or laugh at her. ☐

3 **A** For once, I found myself tongue-tied.
  B For once, I found myself prevented by someone else from expressing my real opinion. ☐

4 **A** I felt underdressed.
  B I felt as if my clothes were too casual compared with everyone else's. ☐

5 **A** That was such an overrated movie.
  B That movie was nothing like as good as most people said it was. ☐

Exercise 6

Put each sentence into the correct order, as shown.

1 trees. / with / was / track / overhanging / darkened / The
   The track was darkened with overhanging trees.

2 were cancelled / hospital / . / the / because / Operations / understaffed / was
   _____

3 In / , / overrated / the / my / band / . / view / is
   _____

4 eat / fish / Never / . / underdone / meat or
   _____

5 underdeveloped / . / depend on / Many / grants / countries
   _____

6 The / was / with / grass / overgrown / path / .
   _____

Exercise 7

Decide if the pairs of sentences have the same meaning.

1 A We couldn't get past because fallen trees blocked the road.
   B We couldn't get past because overgrown trees blocked the road. ☐

2 A Rosa looked very disappointed when she heard that Ben was not coming.
   B Rosa had hoped that Ben was coming, and looked sad to hear that he was not. ☐

3 A The film is about the adventures of escaped zoo animals.
   B The film is about the adventures of animals that have managed to get out of the zoo. ☐

4 A She had an annoying habit of laughing at all her own jokes.
   B She had an annoyed habit of laughing at all her own jokes. ☐

5 A Iwona's new boyfriend is very good-looking.
   B Iwona's new boyfriend looks very nice. ☐

6 A Jorge felt very nervous, but tried to sound light-hearted.
   B Jorge felt very nervous, but tried not to show it. ☐

Adjectives and adverbs

Adjectives and adverbs with different forms and meanings

In this unit you learn to use adjectives and adverbs that have the same form. You also learn to use adverbs that have two forms and meanings and other adverbs that have different meanings depending on their position in a clause.

Adjectives and adverbs that have the same form

Some adverbs of manner have the same form as adjectives and have similar meanings.

> He's always listened to **loud** music.
> The guitarist played too **loud** for the singer's voice to be heard.
> She didn't know what the **right** answer was.
> These are questions that most children get **right**.

These are the most common ones:

direct	right
fast	slow
hard	solo
late	straight
loud	tight
quick	wrong

Adverbs that have a different meaning from their related adjectives

Some **-ly** adverbs have a different meaning from the meanings of their related adjectives. For example, **hardly** means **not very much** or **almost not at all** and is not used with any of the meanings of the adjective **hard**.

> This has been a long **hard** day.
> Her bedroom was so small she could **hardly** move in it.
> Food was **scarce** and so was fuel.
> They could **scarcely** believe their great good fortune.

Here are some adverbs ending in **-ly** that have a different meaning from the meanings of their related adjectives:

barely	presently
hardly	scarcely
lately	shortly

Adverbs with two forms and meanings

Sometimes, two adverbs are related to the same adjective. One adverb has the same form as the adjective, and the other is formed by adding **-ly**.

> There was plenty of room for the children to run **free**.
> Packs of dogs ran **freely**, barking at the cars.
> She woke up in the morning feeling **fine**.
> Peel and **finely** chop the onion.
> The shirt stretched **tight** across his chest.
> Her skin stretched too **tightly** over her cheekbones.
> Marcia opened her eyes **wide**.
> Austria is **widely** regarded as one of the most expensive countries to visit.

Here are some common adverbs that have both these forms:

clear – clearly	hard – hardly
clean – cleanly	high – highly
close – closely	last – lastly
dear – dearly	late – lately
deep – deeply	right – rightly
direct – directly	sharp – sharply
easy – easily	thick – thickly
fine – finely	thin – thinly
first – firstly	tight – tightly
free – freely	wide – widely

Remember!

The **-ly** adverb often has a different meaning from the adverb with the same form as the adjective.

*The water was running **high**.*
*He thought **highly** of his teacher.*
*She worked **hard** all year.*
*We could **hardly** hear him speak.*

Exercise 1

Decide if the pairs of sentences have the same meaning.

1 **A** Would you just give me a direct answer, please? ☐
   B Please answer me immediately.

2 **A** Meet me at 12 sharp. ☐
   B Meet me at precisely 12 o'clock.

3 **A** My late grandmother taught me how to bake. ☐
   B My grandmother, who died two years ago, taught me to bake.

4 **A** You're free to do whatever you want this afternoon. ☐
   B This afternoon's activities are free.

5 **A** We're clean out of salad, I'm afraid. ☐
   B I'm sorry, but we've no salad left at all.

Exercise 2

Which sentences are correct?

1 Fern arrived so lately that her friends had started to worry. ☐

2 The chef chopped the onions and garlic finely before adding them to the hot pan. ☐

3 Our seats were direct in front of the stage so we had a great view of the performers. ☐

4 They arrived at 9 sharp, just as the meeting began. ☐

5 The boy ran past at full speed, close followed by his brother. ☐

6 Right, I've had enough of this. I'm getting out of here. ☐

Exercise 3

Choose the correct word.

1 Her eyes were **wide / widely** open when she was born.

2 He was **right / rightly** annoyed with me for telling everyone his secret.

3 Hold on **tight / tightly**, the train is starting to move.

4 Don't worry – everything will turn out **finely / fine**.

5 He held the book **close / closely** to his chest and refused to let us see it.

6 She didn't speak very **clearly / clear** and I couldn't tell what she was saying.

Exercise 4

Are the highlighted words correct or incorrect in the sentences?

1 Security was very **tight** ☐ during the international athletics competition.

2 The kid came **right** ☐ up to me and stuck his tongue out.

3 It is **wide** ☐ understood that walking here alone at night is best avoided.

4 If you don't look **sharply** ☐ we're going to miss our train.

5 Sara **freely** ☐ admits that she was in the wrong.

6 The chewing gum stuck **fast** ☐ to the sole of my shoe.

Exercise 5

Choose the correct word, as shown.

My friend Lyn has been dating a guy for a few weeks. He swept her ¹**clean** / **cleanly** off her feet at first with romantic meals and flowers, but ²**late / lately** he seems to have cut out the extravagant gestures and I've heard him speak quite ³**sharp / sharply** to her a couple of times, although he always apologizes ⁴**direct / directly** afterwards. It doesn't seem ⁵**right / rightly** to me but maybe I'm being ⁶**over / overly** sensitive about it.

Exercise 6

Choose the correct word.

She looked up ¹**clearly / freely / sharply** as I entered the room. 'What do you want?' she demanded. She was certainly very ²**direct / right / close**, but I'd heard that was her way with newcomers to the firm. 'I wondered if you could show me how to organize the database?' I asked nervously. 'Sit down,' she ordered. I did as I was told, immediately noticing that her chair was much higher than my own. She turned her gaze ³**directly / rightly / tightly** upon me. Her eyes were a ⁴**close / clear / clean**, piercing blue, cold and ⁵**right / fine / sharp** like her manner. 'I'll show you what to do but don't interrupt me while I'm speaking,' she said. My new boss was ⁶**clearly / freely / lately** a woman who didn't like to waste time on pleasantries.

Exercise 7

For each sentence, tick the correct ending.

1 Adam had to go to see the headteacher
   ❑ because he had arrived lately to school.
   ❑ because he had arrived late to school.

2 Ali was ill yesterday,
   ❑ but today he's feeling fine.
   ❑ but today he's feeling finely.

3 Ines was so tired
   ❑ that she could scarce open her eyes.
   ❑ that she could scarcely open her eyes.

4 I hope I am feeling better in time for the wedding,
   ❑ because I would dearly love to go.
   ❑ because I would dear love to go.

5 However hard she tried to hit the ball,
   ❑ Lara couldn't do it rightly.
   ❑ Lara couldn't do it right.

6 Leo did well at school
   ❑ because he always hardly worked.
   ❑ because he always worked very hardly.
   ❑ because he always worked very hard.

Possessive adjectives

Using possessive adjectives and pronouns before *-ing* participles

In this unit you learn to use a possessive adjective or object pronoun before the present participle.

If you want to talk about two closely linked actions that are performed by different people, you follow the first verb with an object. This object then functions as the subject of the second verb. For example:

> *She **saw Brian taking** her diary.*
> *I'd never **caught Sita lying** to me before.*

Brian is the person who is seen. He is also the person who is doing the action of taking her diary.

Sita is the person who is caught. She is also the person who is doing the action of lying.

> *The ball hit Alfie in the chest and **sent him sprawling** to the ground.*
> *Although it's a few years since my mother died, I can still **picture her sitting** at the table.*
> *The look on Maria's face **stopped him saying** anything more.*
> *I could **hear her speaking** to someone on the phone.*

Remember!

When the second verb (or auxiliary) is an *-ing* participle, a possessive adjective is sometimes used in front of it, instead of a pronoun. This is rather formal.

*He did not like **my living** in Paris.*

***His having** been a Goth when he was a teenager came as a surprise to me, since he was now so conventional.*

***The dog's barking** kept me awake all night.*

***Jane's being** unemployed was starting to get me down.*

Some verbs are used with an object and an *-ing* participle in a less formal way.

> *She **observed James walking** down the road.*

You can use these verbs with an object and an *-ing* participle:

catch	keep
describe	leave
feel	like
find	listen to
hear	notice
imagine	observe

picture	spot
prevent	stop
save	want
see	watch
send	

Exercise 1

Put the correct word in each gap.

us | them | His | their | me | her | him

Hi Jamie

How's tricks?

Zoe and I met up with Chaz and Luigi last night. They're great fun. I found out loads about Chaz I didn't know. He was telling us that he'd worked at an elephant orphanage in Sri Lanka for a while. He had [1]_____ all laughing at his stories. He said the elephants would see [2]_____ coming towards them with a cleaning brush and they'd take it from him and run away with it. [3]_____ having worked at such a place surprised me – he likes nothing better than to stay at home watching TV!

Zoe and Chaz seem to be getting on better these days. I watched [4]_____ chatting away like old friends. It used to bother [5]_____, listening to her complain about Chaz being boring. I don't like [6]_____ criticizing my friends – you want everyone to get on well, don't you?

Anyway, speak soon.

Chris

Exercise 2

Match the sentence halves.

1 I don't mind him
2 They spotted us
3 She watched him
4 It bothers me,
5 I can't stand you
6 She worries them,

a going about his daily chores.
b seeing her as long as I don't have to.
c staying out as late as she does.
d nagging at me all the time! Please leave me alone.
e reading the papers in the café.
f hearing him talk about his wife in that way.

Exercise 3

Find the wrong or extra word in each sentence.

1 The baby's crying kept me up all the night.
2 Kate heard him creeping up beside the stairs.
3 She doesn't mind us being here as long as we're remain quiet.
4 Heidi's screaming at the television was getting far on my nerves.
5 Her stealing me the limelight came as no great surprise.
6 I can't bother watch him putting in his contact lenses – urgh!

Exercise 4

Put each sentence into the correct order.

1 her / fired / . / having / lowered / been / self-esteem / Her

_____

2 It / her, / not / allowed / his / to / iPad / borrow / . / bothered / being

_____

3 didn't / not / away / holiday / going / on / She / . / mind

_____

4 us / driveway / up / watched / coming / They / the / . / but / refused / door / to / the / open

_____

5 . / Ernie / her / at / smiled / him / and / saw / looking

_____

6 a / Julio's / being / . / pilot / impressed / Cindy

_____

Exercise 5

Complete the sentences by writing one word in each gap.

1 Her _____ gone blonde gave me the shock of my life!

2 It doesn't bother _____, seeing Emily – it's Greg I can't stand.

3 They caught us spying on _____ from the balcony and waved up at us.

4 I don't _____ you 'borrowing' money from my purse – just ask me first!

5 He heard _____ coughing and went to see if she was OK.

6 Them having bought _____ own car at last was a relief to everyone.

those + participle adjectives

Using *-ing* and *-ed* adjectives with *those*, and in relative clauses

In this unit you learn to use participle adjectives after **those**. You also learn that you can use participle adjectives in relative clauses.

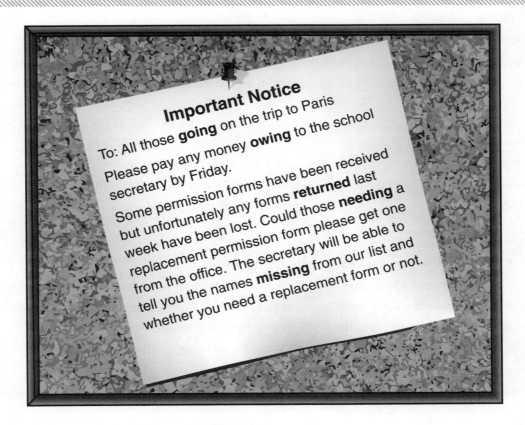

Important Notice

To: All those **going** on the trip to Paris

Please pay any money **owing** to the school secretary by Friday.

Some permission forms have been received but unfortunately any forms **returned** last week have been lost. Could those **needing** a replacement permission form please get one from the office. The secretary will be able to tell you the names **missing** from our list and whether you need a replacement form or not.

Using *-ing* and *-ed* adjectives with *those*

You can use a clause containing an *-ed* participle directly after **those** to show that something or someone has been produced or affected by an action.

> All those **made** of paper quickly caught fire.
> Those **written** before 1900 are very different in style.
> Those **sent** to inpatient care are closely monitored until they are well enough to go home.

You can use a clause containing an *-ing* participle directly after **those** to show that someone or something is doing something.

> All those **going** to London should pay the deposit today.
> Those **containing** errors will be returned immediately for correction.
> Those **making** today's deliveries will start loading at 6 a.m.

Defining relative clauses

You can sometimes reduce a defining relative clause to the **-ed** or **-ing** participle adjective that follows it without changing the meaning. For example:

> We looked through the papers **which were** lying on the table.
> We looked through the papers lying on the table.
> You'll get on well with the man **who'll be** leading your tour.
> You'll get on well with the man leading your tour.
> The decisions **that had been** made by the directors were very poor.
> The decisions made by the directors were very poor.

Exercise 1

Write the correct form of the verb in brackets to complete each sentence, as shown.

1 All those ____*worried*____ (worry) by the plans had an opportunity to voice their concerns.
2 All those _____ (want) to attend the after-school club should put their names on the list.
3 All those _____ (concern) about the new policy should take it up with the Head of Transport.
4 All those _____ (wish) to travel to Cairo, please go to Gate B.
5 All those _____ (intend) to stay for the lecture, please remain seated.
6 All those _____ (affect) by the job cuts will be compensated for their losses.

Exercise 2

Find the wrong or extra word in each sentence, as shown.

1 All those competitors w~~ho~~ remaining in the room have passed the final test – well done!
2 The men were running away from me must have been the ones who'd stolen my money.
3 I couldn't be bothered to open the book that lying on my bedside table.
4 The boy was playing a game on his phone looked up as I sat down next to him.
5 I approached the man who sitting by the entrance door.
6 All those were surprised by the result of the experiment please raise your hands.

Exercise 3

Match the sentence halves.

1 We looked through the papers
2 The decisions
3 You'll get on well with the guide
4 The meal
5 The girl
6 The flowers

a made by the directors caused all the problems.
b growing in the garden looked beautiful.
c being prepared smelled delicious.
d sitting over there is Mike's sister.
e leading the tour.
f lying on the table.

Exercise 4

Decide if the pairs of sentences have the same meaning.

1 A The chef working in the kitchen offered to show us around his workplace. ☐
   B The chef who was working in the kitchen said he would give us a tour of his workplace.

2 A Ted shouted encouragement to the boys running round the field. ☐
   B The boys who were in the field responded to Ted's encouragement by running faster.

3 A Coral nodded to the woman sitting on the bench. ☐
   B Coral nodded to the woman when she sat down on the bench.

4 A The research carried out by our team proved to be inconclusive. ☐
   B The research that our team carried out didn't reach any clear conclusion.

5 A She eyed the last piece of cake left on the plate. ☐
   B She eyed the last piece of cake remaining on the plate.

Exercise 5

Put each sentence into the correct order.

1 girl / the sofa / on / Lucy is / . / the / lying

_____

2 . / were / the wind / by / We / awake / howling / kept / round / the house

_____

3 . / advertised / was / holiday / The / a / great / in the newspaper / bargain

_____

4 a / by / . / complete surprise / delivered / the boy / The message / was

_____

5 under / found / desk / lying / The missing / was / . / cat / my

_____

6 . / teaching / person / today / is / fantastic / The / yoga

_____

Exercise 6

Choose the correct word.

1 The drama **unfolding / unfolded** was watched by tourists in the harbour.

2 Alice has a job **given / giving** guided tours of the city centre to young people.

3 The laws **passed / passing** by the new government were welcomed by most people.

4 All those not **travelling / travelled** to Antigua please leave the ship now.

5 The man **sitting / sat** in front of him had a very large head, so Ethan couldn't see the band.

6 The competition **judging / judged** by the famous photographer had some great prizes.

7

Relative clauses

Whom and *which*

In this unit you learn to use more complex relative clause structures.

Relative pronouns with prepositions

A relative pronoun can be the object of a preposition. The preposition usually goes towards the end of the clause, and not in front of the pronoun.

> ... the job **which** I'd been studying **for**.
> ... the boy **who** Aunt Sophie left her money **to**.
> ... questions **that** there were no answers **to**.

The preposition can go at the beginning of a clause in front of **whom** or **which** but this is usually in more formal English.

> ... the job **for which** I'd been studying.
> ... the boy **to whom** Aunt Sophie left her money.
> ... questions **to which** there were no answers.

> *Remember!*
>
> You cannot put the preposition at the beginning of a clause in front of **who** or **that**.

Relative clause structures introduced by determiners, quantities and superlatives

Words such as **some**, **many** and **most** can be put in front of **of whom** or **of which** at the beginning of a non-defining relative clause.

> A group of men, **all of whom** were armed, surrounded us. These men, **the tallest of whom** was about seven foot, were clearly angry.
> At the door of the hospital we were greeted by the patients, **most of whom** were children.
> There are hundreds of species native to the island, **many of which** are endangered.

Relative clause structures followed by infinitive clauses

An infinitive clause can be put after **of whom**, **of which** or **with which**.

> They wanted money with which **to buy food for their families**.

Exercise 1

Which sentences are correct?

1 I have a new app for my phone which can identify songs that are being played. ❏

2 This is the cottage in what she lived for most of her life. ❏

3 I had three great friends with whom I went travelling in the holidays. ❏

4 I did some gardening for an elderly neighbour, for whom I was paid £6 per hour. ❏

5 We were given plastic cutlery with which to eat our food. ❏

6 There was a large oak tree, under whom we sheltered until the rain had passed. ❏

Exercise 2

Choose the correct word or words.

1 The career for **what / which / that** he had given up so much was now in ruins.

2 She didn't recognize the man **who / whom / which** had spoken.

3 He wanted a companion with **whom / who / which** he could share his love of nature.

4 Each of them were given a pile of wood and some rope with which **construct / constructing / to construct** a raft.

5 **Who / Whom / From whom** gave you the money to buy the car?

6 He wrote extensively about the tribe **from who / from which / from that** he had learned so much.

Exercise 3

Put the correct word in each gap.

writer | confidence | girlfriends | friends | youngest | house

While researching the life of the poet James Arnull, I spoke to several of the ^{1}_____ with whom he grew up in a small Welsh village. All of them remember the energy and ^{2}_____ with which he approached everything in life, from friendship to work to love. Arnull was always a handsome boy, and he had several ^{3}_____, some of whom have found themselves the subject of his poems.

Arnull had three brothers, the ^{4}_____ of whom died at 11 in a car accident – a tragedy that he says has been with him ever since. He lives with Wendy Casey, a Canadian ^{5}_____, with whom he has three children. The large ^{6}_____, to which they moved in 2005, is crammed with souvenirs from their frequent travels to China and Cambodia.

Exercise 4

Complete the sentences by writing one word in each gap.

1 The restaurant may be closed, _____ which case we'll have to cook for ourselves.

2 We came to a building, inside _____ we found a family hiding from the soldiers.

3 He is the friend _____ whom she dedicated her last novel.

4 He handed me the key _____ which to open the case.

5 I called all my friends, none of _____ was able to help.

6 These are matters _____ which I have no control.

Exercise 5

Write the missing words in sentence B so that it means the same as sentence A, as shown.

1 **A** I wrote the poem for him.

   B He is the person ___*for whom*___ I wrote the poem.

2 **A** The house was built on this land.

   B This is the land _____ the house was built.

3 **A** They gave us some money to spend on food.

   B They gave us some money _____ to buy food.

4 **A** Svetlana has six brothers. The oldest is 25.

   B Svetlana has six brothers, the _____ is 25.

5 **A** I bought six peaches, and two of them were rotten.

   B I bought six peaches, two _____ were rotten.

6 **A** Most of Joey's many friends came to his wedding.

   B Joey has many friends, _____ came to his wedding.

Exercise 6

Are the highlighted words correct or incorrect in the sentences?

1 This is a cause **for** ☐ which these men are prepared to die.

2 I talked to some of the athletes, many of **who** ☐ have never competed here before.

3 We were each given a small bag in which **for keeping** ☐ our food.

4 They told me their salaries, most **of whom** ☐ were more than I am likely to earn in my lifetime.

5 We received over 100 stories, the best **of which** ☐ will be published on our website.

6 Five people are accused of the theft, two **of whom** ☐ have already admitted their guilt.

Exercise 7

Are the highlighted words correct or incorrect in this text?

Nature or nurture?

How much of who we are as adults is down to our genes, and how much to our upbringing? Take my neighbours. They have three sons, two of [1]**whom** ❑ are happily married, have stable jobs and have wonderful children of their own. Unfortunately, the third son, [2]**whom** ❑ is much younger, has been nothing but trouble. At the age of 19, he was involved in a robbery, for [3]**what** ❑ he received an 18-month prison sentence.

He was only out for a few months before committing a string of burglaries, [4]**which** ❑ landed him back in jail for another year. His parents, for [5]**which** ❑ I have the greatest respect, have done everything in their power to help him. Nothing has helped. And if he is convicted of the latest crimes of [6]**that** ❑ he is accused, they will have to face the fact that they may not live to see him out of jail again.

Exercise 8

Put each sentence into the correct order.

1 dedicated to / without whom / it could not have / been written / . / The book is / my parents,

_____

2 a special device / . / The dentist / with which / my teeth / gave me / to clean between

_____

3 The folder contains / of people, / is stamped / several photographs / . / on top of which / the word 'traitor'

_____

4 to be known / by which / Ellen is the name / is Elise, but / Her real name / she prefers / .

_____

5 the man / she had been / . / the previous year / living since / with whom / Hoskins was

_____

6 a limit above which / The company pays / we are not / for our hotel and food, / allowed to go / . / but there is

_____

8

Conditionals
Using conditionals to express formality

- **conditional + *if* + *should***
- **conditional + *if* + *were to***
- **inversion of conditionals**

In this unit you learn other ways of using conditionals to express uncertainty and/or formality. You also learn how to form inversion of conditionals by **not** using the **if** conjunction.

Conditionals with *if* + *should*

A more formal way of talking about a possible future situation is to use **should** in the conditional clause. For example, instead of saying *If the letter **arrives** tomorrow, I will reply immediately*, you can say *If the letter **should arrive** tomorrow, I will reply immediately*.

> *If you **should see** him, tell him I called.*
> *If that **should happen**, you will be blamed.*

Conditionals with *if* + *were to*

Another way of talking about a possible future situation is to use **were** and a **to**-*infinitive* in a conditional clause. For example, instead of saying *If you **went** to France next year, I would go too*, you can say *If you **were to go** to France next year, I would go too*.

> *If you **were to marry** him, I would never speak to you again.*
> *If we **were to move** to Nottingham, we would be able to buy a cheaper house.*

Inversion in conditionals

If the first verb in an *if-clause* is **should**, **were** or **had**, this verb is sometimes put at the beginning of the clause and **if** is omitted. For example, you can say ***Should I be** there, I will speak to them* instead of *If **I should be** there, I will speak to them*.

> ***Should ministers demand** an inquiry, we would welcome it.*
> ***Were they to stop** advertising, prices would be significantly reduced.*
> ***Had I known** what you wanted, I'd have called.*
> *You can call our toll-free number, **should you require** assistance.*

> *Remember!*
> Inversion tends to be used in formal or literary English.

Exercise 1

Decide if the pairs of sentences have the same meaning.

1 **A** Were she to ask my opinion, I'd tell her what I think.
  B It's not very likely she'll ask for my opinion, but if she does, I'll tell her. ❏

2 **A** If you were to be elected, what changes would you make?
  B What changes would you have made if you'd been elected? ❏

3 **A** Had I tried harder, I might have done better.
  B I didn't try very hard, so I was lucky to do that well. ❏

4 **A** If the post should come early, can you put it on my desk?
  B The post might come early. If it does, can you put it on my desk? ❏

5 **A** Should you wish to talk to me, you know where I'll be.
  B You know where to find me if by any chance you want to talk to me. ❏

Exercise 2

Choose the correct word.

1 **Were / Should** I to call a meeting, do you think people would come?

2 If the letter **should / would** arrive tomorrow, I'll let you know straight away.

3 **When / Had** I realized you were sick, I would have come to visit you.

4 **Should / Were** Sven decide to come to the festival, I'll book him a ticket.

5 **Were / Had** it not for you, I'd have given up a long time ago.

6 **Should / If** you were to agree to work for us, how many hours could you do?

Exercise 3

Complete the sentences by writing one word in each gap.

| do | would | have | is | did | should | had | are | were |

1 I'd have called back earlier, _____ I known what you wanted.

2 Please contact us in writing, _____ you require any further information.

3 He wouldn't have anything to talk about, _____ it not for his interest in wild flowers.

4 I'll consider accepting the post if the senior managers who interviewed me _____ serious about the project, but I'm not convinced of it.

5 Had you asked Clarissa to go with you, she _____ definitely have said yes.

6 If you should see Amanda, could you tell her the police _____ been looking for her for the last week?

7 I don't expect him to remember that I'm allergic to shellfish – in fact, I'd be amazed if he _____ .

Exercise 4

Are the highlighted words correct or incorrect in the sentences?

1 If I **should** ❏ lend your brother this book, can you make sure I get it back?

2 Were Fiona to invite you to her wedding, what **did** ❏ you say?

3 Had **he** ❏ not been for Kevin, I'd never have passed my driving test.

4 **Had** ❏ you wish to discuss anything further, please don't hesitate to contact me.

5 Had I **known** ❏ that Mary was bringing Pierre with her, I'd have gone out.

6 If Harry **should** ❏ ask you to marry him, would you say yes?

Exercise 5

Which sentences are correct?

1 Weren't it for Angela, I wouldn't be here now. ❏

2 Should anyone wish to join us for a snack, we'll be in the café on the corner. ❏

3 If Nina were come to the party, who do you think she would bring with her? ❏

4 If the car were to break down again, I wouldn't bother trying to fix it yourself. ❏

5 Had I realized you were waiting for me in the hall all that time, I'd get ready more quickly. ❏

6 He'd have refused to pay the builders, had he realized how little work had been done. ❏

Exercise 6

Write the missing words in sentence B so that it means the same as sentence A.

1 **A** If it wasn't for Petra, Amir would never do any travelling.

   B _____ not for Petra, Amir would never do any travelling.

2 **A** If I played this computer game all day, do you think I'd get to the end of it?

   B If I were _____ this computer game all day, do you think I'd get to the end of it?

3 **A** If by any chance the door's locked when you arrive, use this key.

   B Should the door _____ when you arrive, use this key.

4 **A** If I'd known you were coming, I'd have baked a cake!

   B Had _____ you were coming, I'd have baked a cake!

9

Ways of using *as* and *though*

In this unit you learn to use concessive clauses to show a contrast between two statements. You can do this by using an adjective or adverb followed by **as**, **though**, **much as**, **as though**, **as if**, **as for** + noun/pronoun or **as to** + noun.

adjective/adverb + *as* or *though*

though

When a clause beginning with **though** ends with a linking verb like **be** or **seem** and a noun or an adjective (= a complement), you can bring the complement forward to the beginning of the clause. For example, instead of saying *Though he was **tired**, he insisted on coming to the meeting*, you can say ***Tired** though he was, he insisted on coming to the meeting*.

> *Tempting* though it may be to cheat, it is not acceptable.
> I have to believe him, *improbable* though his story is.
> *Astute businessman* though he was, Philip was capable of making mistakes.
> *Strange* though it seems, we have never properly sat down and talked about this issue.
> *Surprising* though it may seem, most fires in people's homes are caused by the careless use of chip pans.

as

When the complement is an adjective, you can use **as** instead of **though**.

> *Stupid* **as** it sounds, I believed her.
> *Charming* as it may be to outsiders, the way of life is one that many people wish to escape.

When a clause beginning with **though** ends with an adverb, you can put the adverb at the beginning of the clause.

> Some members of staff couldn't handle the pressure, *hard* though they tried.

Using *much as*

When you are talking about a strong feeling or desire, you can use **much as** instead of **although**. For example, instead of saying *Although I like Venice, I couldn't live there*, you can say ***Much as** I like Venice, I couldn't live there*.

> *Much as* I like you, I couldn't marry you.
> *Much as* I'd like to go to the cinema, I have to stay in and write my essay.
> *Much as* I hate to admit it, he was right.
> *Much as* they hope to go home tomorrow, they know they have to stay on until the end of the year.

Using *as though* and *as if*

You sometimes want to say that something is done in the way that it *would* be done if something else were the case. You do this by using **as if** or **as though**. You use a past tense in the clause of manner.

> He behaved **as though** he owned the place (= he does not own the place).
> She carried on **as if** nothing had happened (= something has happened).
> She acted **as though** she had no idea who I was (= she does know who I am).
> I put some water on my clothes to make it look **as if** I had been sweating (= I had not been sweating).

Using *as for* + noun/pronoun or *as to* + noun

You can use the prepositional phrases **as for** and **as to** to introduce a new topic or a different aspect of the same topic.

> **As to** what actually happened on that day, there are many differing accounts.
> We will continue to invest in the company. **As for** our staff, they will receive more targeted training.
> He had heard it said that time heals all wounds. **As to** that, he doubted it.
> **As for** what I've told you about last night, we'll keep it quiet as much as possible.

Exercise 1

Match the sentence halves.

1 Much as I'd prefer to come to the concert,
2 Challenging as she may be,
3 Intelligent though she appears,
4 Obvious though it was to everyone else,
5 Much as I like her,
6 Quiet as she is at work,

a she's actually very talkative socially.
b I'm not inviting her to my wedding.
c Mohammed didn't realize Sarah was annoyed with him.
d she didn't do very well in her degree.
e I'm going to ask her to join our team.
f I'm afraid I have to go and watch my daughter's school play.

Exercise 2

Decide if the pairs of sentences have the same meaning.

1 A As for Bruno, I can't see that he'll ever make it as a professional footballer. ☐
  B Bruno is unlikely ever to play football for a professional team.
2 A He's a very demanding boss, nice though he is. ☐
  B He would be a nice boss if he expected less of his staff.
3 A I'd like to go camping this weekend. Whether I'll actually go depends on whether I finish my work. ☐
  B If I finish my work, I'll go camping this weekend.
4 A Ruby's vegetarian and loves fresh vegetables. As for her husband, he can't stand them. ☐
  B Ruby's husband is as keen as Ruby to eat fresh vegetables.
5 A Tired as I am, I'm still coming clubbing with you! ☐
  B I'm tired, but I am going clubbing with you even so.

Exercise 3

Complete the sentences by writing one word in each gap.

1 As _____ you – be quiet while I'm talking!

2 Carol has pizza practically every night. As _____ me, I hate the stuff.

3 Unlucky _____ it was, Bob failed his 17th driving test.

4 Stop behaving as _____ the world owes you something!

5 I've booked our flights. _____ to the hotel, I can't find one I like.

6 _____ as I'd like the weather to brighten up, it's looking unlikely.

Exercise 4

Choose the correct word.

1 As **to / for** Gina, I don't know where she got to.

2 They behaved as **if / for** they owned the place!

3 The parents ate out every night. As **to / for** the kids, they made their own meals.

4 As **to / though** the cause of the row – I've no idea what started it.

5 Milena's always sticking her nose in. It's as **though / to** she can't bear to be left out.

6 Nelly always stays in at the weekend. As **to / for** her husband, he goes out with his friends.

Exercise 5

Which sentences are correct?

1 Weird though it sounds, I can only sleep during the day. ❏

2 As to you, get back indoors! You've nothing on your feet! ❏

3 It's as if she thinks I'm her personal slave, the way she orders me about! ❏

4 She acts as though she's never seen me before, yet I walk past her on Reception every day. ❏

5 As she seems friendly, I wouldn't want to get on the wrong side of her. ❏

6 Childish though they are, I love practical jokes. ❏

Exercise 6

Write the missing word or words in sentence B so that it means the same as sentence A.

1 **A** She can be funny but she can be serious as well.

B Funny _____ can be, she has a serious side too.

2 **A** I must get an early night tonight, even though I'd really like to see you.

B _____ as I'd like to see you tonight, I must have an early night.

3 **A** The bus was late because of the traffic. But I really don't know why it broke down.

B The bus was late because of the traffic. But _____ the reason it broke down – I've no idea.

4 **A** Michael was exhausted after the long trip but Emma was keen to explore.

B Michael was exhausted after the long trip. As _____, she was keen to explore.

10

Using *it* as an object in sentences

it + adjective/noun + clause

it + person/institution + *to-infinitive*

In this unit you learn to use **it** in a number of ways.

To: Belle
From: Helen
Subject: Phil's birthday

Hey Belle!

How's life? I've been really busy recently, what with organising Phil's 40th birthday party. I'm not keen on organising stuff because I **find it a bit stressful**. I **think it'd be easier** if I had someone to help me out with it but I want it to be a surprise so I'm keeping it to myself for now. My biggest problem is knowing who to invite. Phil won't **like it** if I forget anyone important. So I'm going through his address book to make sure I **get it right**.

You know my brother's a DJ? I'm going to **leave it to him to sort out** the music – he knows what Phil likes.

Hopefully I can **make it a party to remember**! Watch out for your invite in the post.

Helen
xx

it after *find, think, make,* etc.

After verbs like **find** and **think**, you can use **it** as the object, followed by an adjective, and either a **to**-*infinitive* or a **that**-*clause*.

> I **found it strange** that he kept silent.
> The thick snow **made it difficult** to see very far in front of me.

it after *see, regard,* etc.

After verbs like **see**, **take** and **regard,** you can use **it** as the object, followed by **as**, followed by an adjective or noun and a clause.

> They'll **regard it as insulting** if we don't accept the present.
> He **saw it as a sign** that things were about to improve.

it after *like, love, hate,* etc.

After verbs like **love**, **like** and **hate**, you can use **it** as the object, followed by a clause with **when** or **that**.

> My cat **loves it** when you stroke her neck.
> I **hate it** when Jane keeps me waiting.
> They didn't **like it** that we refused their invitation.

Here are some more verbs that are used in this way:

adore	like
dislike	loathe
enjoy	love
hate	prefer

it after *owe* and *leave*

After verbs like **owe** and **leave**, you can use **it** as the object, followed by a person/institution and **to**-*infinitive*.

> *I'll **leave it to you to choose** which cake we have.*
> *You **owe it to your country to work** as hard as you can.*

Exercise 1

Match the sentence halves.

1 The rail strike made it   **a** as rude if you don't go with him.

2 You owe it   **b** to you to decide what music to play.

3 I'll leave it   **c** when you leave wet towels on the floor.

4 She thought it   **d** impossible for me to get home.

5 I hate it   **e** to your team to play as well as you can.

6 He'll see it   **f** odd that he hadn't contacted her.

Exercise 2

Which sentences are correct?

1 They didn't like we turned down their invitation. ☐

2 She'll regard it as an insult if we don't accept her generosity. ☐

3 The baby loves when you tickle her tummy! ☐

4 I found it strange that he stayed silent throughout the meeting. ☐

5 He saw as a sign that things were about to take a turn for the better. ☐

6 We'll leave it to the children to decide what games to play at the party. ☐

Exercise 3

Complete the sentences by writing one word in each gap.

find	take	make	love	hate	have	owe	do

1 You _____ it to your brother to apologize for interrupting his meeting.

2 I _____ it when my wife comes home late from work, as I worry that something's happened to her.

3 My sister will _____ it as a personal affront if I don't go to her party.

4 You sometimes _____ it very difficult for me to get my point across.

5 Jude will _____ it odd that there's nobody at home when he gets back from his trip.

6 My children _____ it when their grandparents play with them, and keep demanding more.

Exercise 4

Put each sentence into the correct order.

1 it / difficult / me / made / for / He / . / the job offer / to refuse

_____

2 it / upsetting / I / dismissed / to be / found / . / by text message

_____

3 . / We / it / when / compliments / we receive / like / all

_____

4 it / leaves / his / organize / . / their / social life / to / wife / Bob / to

_____

5 it / yourself / to / owe / hard / You / . / to work

_____

6 sees / as / it / insulting / him / incorrectly / . / if / people / address / He

_____

Exercise 5

Complete the sentences by writing one word in each gap.

1 The traffic jam made _____ impossible for me to arrive on time.

2 She sees it _____ her right to do whatever she wants.

3 Lara takes it very badly _____ she loses a match.

4 When she phoned, he took it _____ a sign that he was forgiven.

5 You owe it _____ yourself to do well in your exams.

6 He always _____ it to me to clear up after a meal, which I find very annoying.

Exercise 6

For each sentence, tick the correct ending.

1 Looking around the room,
  ❑ Lena thought it strange to be few personal photographs.
  ❑ Lena thought it strange that there were few personal photographs.

2 The bright torch
  ❑ made easier to see in the thick fog.
  ❑ made it easier to see in the thick fog.

3 When I said you had a very relaxed attitude,
  ❑ I didn't mean you to take it as a criticism.
  ❑ I didn't mean you to take it for a criticism.

4 Clara was so bored with her work that, when the doorbell rang,
  ❑ she saw it a welcome interruption.
  ❑ she saw it as a welcome interruption.

5 When I met her for the first time,
  ❑ I thought it surprising that she already knew my name.
  ❑ I thought it surprising to already know my name.

6 Both websites contain a section on this topic and
  ❑ you may find it interesting in comparing the two.
  ❑ you may find it interesting to compare the two.

11

Using comparative structures for cause and effect

The sooner, the better

the + a comparative adjective, adverb or noun, _the_ + a comparative adjective, adverb or noun or verb

In this unit you learn to use the comparative structure **the** + a comparative adjective, adverb or noun to show simultaneous cause and effect.

The more birds the cat eats, **the fatter** the cat will get.

You can show that one amount of a quality or thing is linked to another amount by using two contrasted comparatives preceded by **the**.

__The longer__ we stay, __the harder__ it will be to leave.
__The more__ the atoms vibrate, __the hotter__ the wire becomes.
__The less__ I see of him, __the better__.
__The more__ I find out about her, __the less__ I want to get to know her.

> ## Remember!
> The two clauses have a comma between them.

Exercise 1

Match the sentence halves.

1 The braver the bird,
2 The greater the artist,
3 The bigger they are,
4 The worse the wedding,
5 The colder the winter,
6 The harder the battle,

a the greater the paintings.
b the sweeter the victory.
c the better the marriage.
d the warmer the spring.
e the harder they fall.
f the fatter the cat.

Exercise 2

Put each sentence into the correct order.

1 . / the / I / learn / , / more / I / less / know / The

_____

2 , / the / it / darker / The / is / . / harder / to / it / see / is

_____

3 . / chicken / the / the / , / fox / the / fatter / The / bigger

_____

4 the / sleep / less / , / I / . / tired / more / I / The / become

_____

5 the / rains / , / The / it / more / . / it / likelier / to / is / flood

_____

6 . / the / colder / The / it / less / I / is / , / want / to / out / go

_____

Exercise 3

Which sentences are correct?

1 The hungrier I am, the more I'm eating. ❏
2 The harder I work, the luckier I become. ❏
3 The sooner we get there, sooner we can leave. ❏
4 The more exercise I do, the fitter I get. ❏
5 The less I see of Mickey, the better. ❏
6 The longer we stay, the harder is it to leave. ❏

Exercise 4

Complete the sentences by writing one word in each gap. The first letter of the word has already been added.

1 The more I see him, the m_____ I want to – he's lovely!
2 The more work I have to do, the l_____ I want to do it – it's so boring!
3 The more money I make, the w_____ I become.
4 The funnier she is, the h_____ I laugh.
5 The more he eats, the f_____ he becomes.
6 The more they persist, the more a_____ I become.

Exercise 5

Find the wrong or extra word in each sentence.

1 The louder they shout, the less I want to listen them.

2 The more passionately they argue, the less I inclined believe them.

3 The more time I have, the less I seem to get more done.

4 The bigger is my handbag, the more I find to put in it.

5 The faster I pedal, the sooner I will be reach my destination.

6 The more money I make, the more I can donate it to others.

Exercise 6

Decide if the pairs of sentences have the same meaning.

1 **A** The more she thought about it, the more she realized that she had been wrong.
  B Thinking about it more made her convinced that she had been wrong. ☐

2 **A** The more freedom the children have, the more dangers they will face.
  B The children are dangerous when they are given more freedom. ☐

3 **A** The greater the height, the greater the fall.
  B Being higher up means that there is further to fall. ☐

4 **A** The less he spoke, the more he heard.
  B He couldn't hear very well when he was speaking. ☐

5 **A** The harder Petra tried to put things right, the worse the problems became.
  B Petra trying to put things right made the problems worse. ☐

6 **A** The less sugar you put in the dessert, the healthier it will be.
  B Sugar is healthier when you put it in a dessert. ☐

Exercise 7

For each sentence, tick the correct ending.

1 The less the teacher knows
  ☐ about what you have been doing, better.
  ☐ about what you have been doing, the better.

2 The faster Emma ran,
  ☐ the harder her heart pumped.
  ☐ her heart pumped harder.

3 The more he learned about them,
  ☐ he felt he knew them better.
  ☐ the better he felt he knew them.

4 The hotter the climate,
  ☐ the higher the sun protection you will need.
  ☐ the higher you will need sun protection.

5 The more space you have,
  ☐ the easier is it to exercise indoors.
  ☐ the easier it is to exercise indoors.

6 The less you earn,
  ☐ the less you will pay in tax.
  ☐ less you will pay in tax.

12

Using *-ing* clauses after certain verbs

verb + object + *-ing* clause

In this unit you learn to use complementary *-ing* clauses after certain verbs. Many of these verbs are about our senses.

| To: Sandy |
| From: Dan |
| Subject: Leather factory |

Hi Sandy

How are you? What have you been up to?

I went to a leather factory yesterday as part of my course. It was very smelly and noisy.

When you went in you could **hear the workers cutting** animal skins into regular sizes on machines. Then we moved on to the next part of the process and you could **smell the skins boiling** in some sort of solution – it was disgusting! Mind you, I usually find visiting factories boring – this certainly wasn't!

Anyway, when we got to the end of the process and I **touched some leather lying** on a workbench, it was like silk – so soft and delicate.

The guy taking us round explained that there are lots of different qualities of leather and he **got us grading** some samples. He was really good at promoting the industry; he **had us all seriously considering** it as a career option.

And you never know, I might go into it.

See you
Dan

You can use an *-ing* clause after certain verbs plus an object.

> *I **smelt the roses growing** outside the window.*
> *Did you **watch the children playing** football?*
> *I **found them having** an argument.*
> *She'll **get everyone talking** to each other.*

There are a number of verbs that can be used in this type of clause.

Many of them are verbs about our senses:

hear	listen to
feel	notice
smell	watch

However, there are other verbs that can also be used in this way:

find	catch
get	leave
have	

Exercise 1

For each sentence, tick the correct ending.

1 The film was so funny,
- ❏ it had ourselves crying with laughter.
- ❏ it had to cry with laughter.
- ❏ it had us crying with laughter.

2 It's so lovely to have
- ❏ flowers that growing in the garden.
- ❏ flowers growing in the garden.
- ❏ flowers grew in the garden.

3 I found my sister, who claims never to eat cake,
- ❏ cutting herself a huge slice of cheesecake.
- ❏ having cutting a huge slice of cheesecake.
- ❏ cutting her a huge slice of cheesecake.

4 How do you find
- ❏ living in that remote farmhouse?
- ❏ to live in that remote farmhouse?
- ❏ live that remote farmhouse?

5 Nancy always gets
- ❏ talking everyone to each other at parties.
- ❏ everyone talking to each other at parties.
- ❏ everyone talking each other at parties.

6 I eventually managed to get
- ❏ the clock working again.
- ❏ the clock worked again.
- ❏ the clock works again.

Exercise 2

Match the sentence halves.

1 I smelt the sausages
2 I heard the children
3 I saw the ship
4 I touched the old man
5 I felt the wind
6 I tasted the sweetness of the sugar

a sleeping on the bench to wake him up.
b coating the doughnut.
c leaving on its last voyage.
d grilling on the barbecue.
e giggling in the kitchen.
f blowing through my hair.

Exercise 3

Write the correct form of the verb in brackets to complete each sentence.

1 Do you find _____ (go) to work by train quicker than by car?
2 See that man _____ (wear) a white shirt? That's my new neighbour.
3 I found the children _____ (play) in the garden.
4 You've got me _____ (worry) about where my mobile phone is.
5 I can't smell the onions _____ (fry): have you turned the gas on?
6 Get all the children _____ (sit) down before you start the lesson.

Exercise 4

Find the wrong or extra word in each sentence.

1 You've got me to thinking I might apply for that job.
2 Could you watch the children who playing in the garden while I cook dinner?
3 I can hear it the man in the flat above playing the violin every weekend.
4 Please get everyone themselves sitting down before you make the announcement.
5 How do you find to working in such a small office?
6 Can you see the bird with white tail feathers that feeding by the gate?

Exercise 5

Which sentences are correct?

1 My sports coach has got me running ten kilometres twice a week now. ❏
2 A lot of people find that saving for the future very hard to do. ❏
3 From my hotel window I could hear the waves crashing on the shore during the storm. ❏
4 Do you think you could get my old watch works? ❏
5 Can you see that woman in a red dress dancing with Stephen? ❏
6 How do you find to study in the new library? ❏

Exercise 6

Decide if the pairs of sentences have the same meaning.

1 **A** We sat on the patio and listened to the children playing in the garden.
  B We sat on the patio and heard the sounds that the children made as they played in ☐ the garden.

2 **A** My parents will be angry if they catch us borrowing their car. ☐
  B My parents will be angry if they chase us in their car.

3 **A** His remark had me thinking that it would be nice to go on holiday. ☐
  B He remarked that he thought it would be nice to go on holiday.

4 **A** Mia could smell the hot dogs and hamburgers cooking on the open grill. ☐
  B The smell of the hot dogs and hamburgers on the open grill reached Mia.

5 **A** I watched her putting on her coat and leaving the house. ☐
  B I watched her as she put on her coat and left the house.

6 **A** His mother left him filling out the application form. ☐
  B When his mother left, he was filling out the application form.

Exercise 7

Put each sentence into the correct order.

1 living / How / the countryside / ? / she find / in / does / out

_____

2 had / all / . / Zoe / laughing / us / soon

_____

3 catch / You / wearing / a / me / won't / . / bikini

_____

4 blowing / the trees / We / could / the wind / . / hear / through

_____

5 noticed them / to / during / each other / talking / Leo / . / the break

_____

6 brushing against / her face / in the darkness / something / . / Michelle / could feel

_____

13

Focusing sentences (1)

Using *it*

it + be

In this unit you learn to use focusing sentences with **it**.

One way of focusing on a particular part of a sentence is to use a split sentence. This involves using the verb **be**, either with **it** as an impersonal subject or with a clause such as a relative clause or a **to**-*infinitive* clause.

If you want to emphasize one noun phrase, you can use **It is** or **It was** and follow it with a relative clause. For example, instead of saying *Sarah gave the right answer,* you may want to stress the fact that Sarah did it by saying **It was Sarah** *who gave the right answer.* In the next two sentences, you can see how you can use **It is** or **It was** to focus on different parts of the sentence:

> **It was** *Colin who married my sister.*
> **It was** *my sister that Colin married.*

Similarly, instead of saying *Betty makes cakes,* you can say **It's** *cakes that Betty makes.*

> **It's** *food that he wants.*
> **It's** *younger children that Maria most enjoys teaching.*
> **It's** *money that he needs, not advice.*
> **It was** *his sense of humour that she missed the most.*

> *Remember!*
>
> In some cases, the **that** in the **that**-*clause* can be omitted.
> *It's money he needs, not advice.*

In a split sentence, you usually focus on a noun phrase. However, you can focus on other clause elements or even on a whole clause. You then use a relative clause beginning with **that**.

In order to stress the circumstances of an event, you can make a prepositional phrase, a time adverbial or an adverb of place the focus of a split sentence.

> **It was** *from her dad* **that** *she first learned to drive.*
> *Could* **it have been** *then* **that** *I first realized I was in love?*
> **It was** *in London* **that** *I met my first boyfriend.*
> **Was it** *then* **that** *you decided to become a lawyer?*

You can also focus on an **-ing** form if you are stressing an action.

> **It was getting** *a car that really started me off on my career.*
> **It was seeing** *the expressions on the faces of the patients that persuaded me.*
> **It was going** *to South America as a teenager that made Anya love travelling.*

You can focus on a clause beginning with **because** to stress the reason for something.

*Perhaps **it's because** we're from the same place that we get on so well with each other.*
***It is because** you are there that your child can sleep peacefully after an operation.*
*I suppose **it was because** she didn't ask for money that I offered it.*

Exercise 1

Match the sentence halves.

1 It was Klaus who

2 It's this car

3 Could it have been at Sam's party

4 Is it on Saturday

5 I like Madrid a lot,

6 No, it was in May

a but it's Paris that I like the best.

b we're playing tennis?

c we went on holiday.

d won the Business Person of the Year award.

e Ivan bought, not that one.

f that you met Pilar?

Exercise 2

Put each sentence into the correct order.

1 the / who / was / . / won / Martin / It / prize

_____

2 cinema / It's / the / Saturday / . / going / we're / to

_____

3 June / we / ten / married / It'll / . / got / in / since / be / years

_____

4 doesn't / machine / ? / be / can / work / this / it / How / still / that

_____

5 who / sent / Simon / the / have / been / card / it / Could / Valentine's / ?

_____

6 whether / July / don't / move / will / know / be / that / it / I / we / in / .

_____

Exercise 3

Put the correct word in each gap.

| that's | not | who | wasn't | there | who's | it | been |

Hi Ellie

I'm thinking of going to the Lake District on holiday and I seem to remember [1]_____
was just last year that you went there. I think you said you booked a cottage to rent through a
website. It [2]_____ www.lakes42.co.uk that you used, was it? Or could it have
[3]_____ BandBLakes.com? It's my sister Julie [4]_____ really wants to go
there rather than me – she loves sailing. I really wanted to go to a city but it's [5]_____
me who gets to choose this year, it's Julie's turn. Would you say it's autumn [6]_____
the best time to go to the lakes? What would you recommend?

Love

Anna

Exercise 4

Decide if the pairs of sentences have the same meaning.

1 A Could it have been in London that you saw Phil?
   B Could it have been Phil that you saw in London? ☐

2 A It's Mike who's going to do the presentation tomorrow, not Simon.
   B Simon is the one who's going to do the presentation tomorrow instead of Mike. ☐

3 A It'll be two years in January since we opened this restaurant.
   B We opened this restaurant two years ago in January. ☐

4 A It's those black boots next to the red shoes that I'd like to try on.
   B I'd like to try on the black boots first and then the red shoes. ☐

5 A I'm sure it was this report on population growth that had a section missing.
   B I'm sure the report on population growth has been corrected. ☐

6 A Why is it always me who gets asked to work late?
   B I'm fed up with always being asked to work late. ☐

Exercise 5

Are the highlighted words correct or incorrect in the sentences?

1 It ☐ is Jane who should complain, not us.

2 It was in Rio de Janeiro **who** ☐ I learned to dance the samba.

3 Who is it **that** ☐ you wish had won the competition?

4 Do you think **they're** ☐ the 500-metre race that's the most difficult for her?

5 It couldn't have **been** ☐ the manager who stole the money, surely!

6 I don't think it was a Friday **which** ☐ we flew to Sydney.

Exercise 6

Which sentences are correct?

1 Is it this box that you'd like me to carry upstairs for you? ☐

2 How can it be that I haven't got my visa yet? ☐

3 Could it have had in New York that you first ate sushi? ☐

4 It's me which will have to take the blame. ☐

5 It'll be the kitchen who we redecorate first, and then the bathroom. ☐

6 Was it Jamie who put these flowers on my desk? ☐

14

Focusing sentences (2)

Using *what*

what + be

In this unit you learn to use focusing sentences with **what** referring to the object or the subject.

Study skills

Welcome to course DD101.

What you need to do first is to read the study companion.

On 4 October, **what you must do is register** online. You can then access all the course material. **What has been a problem** in the past is the students forgetting their password, so write it down somewhere safe.

On the website, **what you should look at** and make a copy of **is** the study schedule. **What this tells you is** the term dates and all your assignment dates. If you think you won't be able to meet an assignment deadline, **what you must do is inform** us straight away.

If you want to focus on an action performed by someone, you can use a split sentence consisting of **what** followed by the subject, the verb **do**, the verb **be** and an infinitive with or without **to**. For example, instead of saying *I called Polly immediately*, you can say ***What I did was to call Polly immediately***.

> ***What you have to do is** to choose your courses for next year.*

Clauses with **what** as their subject are sometimes used to focus on the thing you are talking about. They can be put after the verb **be** as well as in front of it. For example, you can say *His idealism was what caught my attention*, as well as *What caught my attention was his idealism*.

> ***What annoyed me most was** their dishonesty.*
> *These topic areas **are what constitute** this week's lessons.*

If you want to focus on the thing that someone wants, needs or likes, you can use a split sentence beginning with a clause consisting of **what** followed by the subject and a verb such as **want** or **need**. After this clause, you use the verb **be** and a noun phrase referring to the thing wanted, needed or liked. For example, instead of saying *We need a bigger garden*, you can say **What we need is** a bigger garden.

What he wanted was a cup of tea.
What you need is a dentist.

Here is a list of verbs that can be used with **what** in this structure:

adore	loathe
dislike	love
enjoy	need
hate	prefer
like	want

> ### Remember!
> If you do not want to mention the performer, you can use a passive form of the verb.
> **What's needed is** patience.

Exercise 1

Match the sentence halves.

1 What you could add to your essay
2 What I'd like to know is
3 What she's chosen to do is
4 What this company does
5 What we couldn't understand was
6 What this soup could do with

a is sell cosmetics online.
b why she hadn't told us first.
c is a little more salt.
d is more examples.
e how are we going to get home?
f study fashion design.

Exercise 2

Are the highlighted words correct or incorrect in the sentences?

1 What I can't understand **is** ☐ how you managed to save so much money.
2 What she **did** ☐ now is work part-time for a charity.
3 What we had forgotten **was** ☐ to take an umbrella.
4 What we **do** ☐ is invest in small IT companies.
5 What Frank **wants** ☐ is less responsibility.
6 What **have** ☐ been stolen is my wallet.

Exercise 3

Find the wrong or extra word in each sentence.

1 What happens is, when you fill out the application form and they contact you by email.

2 What you do with is your own business.

3 What I tend to do is that smile, nod and pretend I understand.

4 What works is to holding your nose and counting to 20.

5 What I couldn't understand about was why they hadn't phoned.

6 What does surprises me most is that she's achieved so much and yet she's still only 21.

Exercise 4

Write the missing word or words in sentence B so that it means the same as sentence A.

1 **A** I don't know why they decided to do it today.

  B _____ I don't know is why they decided to do it today.

2 **A** He bought a small gold chain.

  B _____ a small gold chain.

3 **A** She sells antiques.

  B _____ sell antiques.

4 **A** Concrete evidence is lacking.

  B _____ is concrete evidence.

5 **A** He'll announce his decision at the weekly meeting.

  B What _____ announce his decision at the weekly meeting.

6 **A** I tried adding more sugar to the recipe.

  B _____ more sugar to the recipe.

Exercise 5

Complete the sentences by writing one word in each gap.

1 What I need right now _____ a vacation.

2 What I said _____ 'Put it on the bottom shelf'.

3 What she _____ was turn off all the electricity.

4 What _____ gone missing was the file on James Bond.

5 What I _____ realize at the time was that the dessert contained coffee. I would never have guessed.

6 _____ is puzzling me is, why didn't he lock the door?

15

Using *to-infinitive* clauses as subject/object

In this unit you learn to use **to**-*infinitive* clauses as subject or object.

You can place a **to**-*infinitive* clause after nouns in order to show what the thing referred to is intended to do.

*The government set up a programme **to develop new varieties of corn**.*
*We need employees **to work in the new call centre**.*
*They gave me a call **to check if I would consider rejoining the team**.*
*He was looking for someone **to organize the tennis tournament**.*

You can refer to something or someone that should or can have something done to them by using a clause containing a **to**-*infinitive* after a noun or indefinite pronoun.

*I make lists in the front of my diary of things **to be bought**.*
*She recruited local people **to be trained** in Hong Kong.*
*There were fences **to be mended** and tiles **to be repaired**.*

You can use a clause consisting of a **to**-*infinitive* followed by a preposition.

*There wasn't even a chair **to sit on**.*
*He had nothing **to write with**.*
*Leila was glad to have someone **to talk to**.*
*At least we now have a goal **to aim at**.*
*She had everything in the world **to live for**.*

A **to**-*infinitive* clause can be used when you want to say what you are talking about, for example, the *first*, *oldest*, or *only* person who did something. For example

*Maureen Stuart was **the first woman to be elected** to the council.*
*Reagan had become, at seventy-four, **the oldest man ever to hold** the presidency.*
*Of the seven children born to the Gibbons, Edward was **the only one to survive** to adulthood.*

A clause containing a **to**-*infinitive* is used after some abstract nouns to show what action they relate to.

*Adults who didn't have **the chance to go to school** when they were children can go to night school.*
*She resisted **the desire to let her eyes close** again.*
*Idoia welcomed **any opportunity to practise** her English.*

Exercise 1

Match the sentence halves.

1 Javier is happy with his life; he wants
2 John likes horses but doesn't know
3 Elsa hasn't booked a holiday yet because she hasn't decided
4 There's a party at a club in town tonight and I've invited
5 The sports centre also provides
6 Flat-hunting is hard work, but if I don't hurry I'll never find

a where to go.
b nothing about it to change.
c somewhere to eat and drink.
d a place to live.
e how to ride.
f loads of friends from college to come.

Exercise 2

Decide if the pairs of sentences have the same meaning.

1 A For Jim to be so friendly was a rare event.
  B Jim is not often so friendly.

2 A The desire to go surfing suddenly left him.
  B He suddenly lost the desire to go surfing.

3 A She felt a sudden need to laugh, despite the serious situation.
  B The situation was so serious that she couldn't laugh.

4 A All the children left of the meal was a mess to clear up.
  B Every child helped clear up the mess after the meal.

Exercise 3

Write the simple past form of the verb in brackets to complete each sentence.

1 The only thing I need now is something _____ (drink).
2 Books to read on the beach _____ (be) selling well at the moment.
3 It must be hard to find a place _____ (stay) when you're in the jungle.
4 The plan to build a skate park in Morley Park _____ (be) announced a few hours ago by the city council.
5 I live a long way from my mum and I miss having her _____ (talk) to.
6 On the first day of the course, Selma _____ (not know) where to go for classes but she soon found out.

Exercise 4

Put each sentence into the correct order.

1 dolphins / in their / To see / . / natural environment / magical / was
_____

2 is on / page 45 / The text / to read for homework / .
_____

3 to look after / sick / . / The hospital / needs / two nurses / children
_____

4 anyone / doesn't / Stefan / to sit / in his seat / . / like
_____

5 so much / To win / make / would / happy / . / anyone / money
_____

6 was what / this moment / . / he / Something tasty / wanted most at / to eat
_____

Exercise 5

For each sentence, tick the correct ending.

1 I need to go clothes shopping because I haven't got anything
   ❏ wearing.
   ❏ wear.
   ❏ to wear.

2 To swim in the Norwegian sea in winter
   ❏ is madness!
   ❏ being madness!
   ❏ and it's madness!

3 What I'm looking for is a good film
   ❏ to watch.
   ❏ do you watch?
   ❏ like watching.

4 A tent we could carry on our bikes
   ❏ is the whole trip.
   ❏ were very light.
   ❏ was difficult to find.

5 To be so beautiful
   ❏ is being wonderful.
   ❏ must be great.
   ❏ she is happy.

Exercise 6

For each sentence, tick the correct ending.

1 Harriet is
   ❏ the first girl at our school to win a scholarship.
   ❏ the first girl at our school who wins a scholarship.

2 Mario enjoys being outdoors and loves
   ❏ an opportunity of playing sport.
   ❏ any chance to play sport.

3 They all did well at school,
   ❏ but Rita was the only one to go to university.
   ❏ but Rita was only one who went to university.

4 We've sold our house, but
   ❏ we haven't found a house that we can move yet.
   ❏ we haven't found a house to move into yet.

5 The company often sends employees on courses
   ❏ to learn new skills.
   ❏ for learn new skills.

6 You must be thirsty – Would you
   ❏ want to drink of anything?
   ❏ like anything to drink?

Exercise 7

Decide if the pairs of sentences have the same meaning.

1 **A** They are looking for a person to answer the phone and deal with all the correspondence.
    B They are hoping to employ someone who will answer the phone and deal with all the correspondence. ❑

2 **A** Giuseppe gave Manda a call to check if she was coming to the party.
    B Giuseppe phoned Manda because he wanted to know if she was coming to the party. ❑

3 **A** My boss presented me with a list of things to be done.
    B My boss showed me all that he had to do. ❑

4 **A** On the school trip, Tanja was given six children to look after.
    B Six children went on the school trip with Tanja. ❑

5 **A** To come first in the race would be a great achievement for Youssef.
    B Youssef achieved a great thing by coming first in the race. ❑

6 **A** There's lots to be done in preparation for the wedding.
    B There are lots of jobs to do to prepare for the wedding. ❑

Exercise 8

Put the correct word or words in each gap.

save	consider	to save	do	to do	to help	help	to consider

Do you think you could start your own business one day? If so, then ¹_____ what people will want to buy is a good starting point in the process.

For example, ideas ²_____ people money are always popular, so ³_____ selling a product that can do this. Similarly, products which ⁴_____ people time are likely to be good sellers. Most people are also keen to learn how ⁵_____ new things, so products that enable this are likely to succeed. Finally, customers are very interested in products that can improve their health: creating something ⁶_____ people sleep or feel more relaxed may be your first step to making yourself a fortune!

16

Using negatives with reporting verbs

think, expect, believe and *seem*

In this unit you learn to use negatives with reporting verbs such as **think**, **expect**, **believe**, **seem**, etc. This is called transferred negation. You also learn when transferred negation is not used.

Reporting verbs with a negative

With a small number of reporting verbs, you usually make the reporting clause negative rather than the reported clause. For example, you would usually say I **don't think** Mary is at home rather than I think Mary **is not** at home.

> **Don't you suppose** he's heard the news already?
> **He doesn't believe** that I'll win.
> **They don't seem** to be expecting us.
> **I don't imagine** it is possible to have a successful club without a good manager.
> **I do not expect** that we will have a balanced budget in this current financial year.
> **She didn't think** that it was Mohammed's fault.

The following reporting verbs are often used with a negative in this way.

believe	reckon
expect	seem
feel	suppose
imagine	think
propose	

Reporting verbs where negation can't be transferred

With other verbs it is the reported clause that takes the negative form. The reporting verb stays in the positive and the negative cannot be transferred. You usually say I assume you **haven't heard**, NOT ~~I don't assume you have heard~~.

> I hope the euro **doesn't get** any weaker.
> I suspect we **won't hear** from him again.
> She promised she **would never do** it again.
> I would guess she **didn't profit** that much.
> They concluded that death **was not** due to natural causes.
> The doctor predicted that she **would never run** again.

The following reporting verbs are examples of verbs *not* used in the negative.

accept	deny
admit	feel
agree	guess
allege	hope
argue	predict
assume	presume
claim	promise
concede	stress
conclude	suggest
confess	suspect
declare	

> *Remember!*
>
> Usually the **that** in the **that**-*clause* is not used.
> *I guess ~~that~~ the minister won't retire.*

Exercise 1

Match the sentence halves.

1 It's rumoured that management aren't too impressed with him. I don't reckon

2 He looks pretty laid back. I don't imagine

3 She's in the office till 9 o'clock most evenings. I don't suppose

4 He's pretty lean. I don't imagine

5 He's quite an attractive guy. I don't suppose

6 She doesn't seem very keen on him. I don't reckon

a he'll be in this company too much longer.

b he has any trouble getting dates.

c that relationship's going to last.

d there's too much stress in his life.

e she sees too much of her kids.

f he eats too many burgers.

Exercise 2

Complete the sentences by writing one phrase in each gap.

she even knows who I am | she even needs to work | she ever diets | she is
she will | she does

1 Camilla inherited so much money when her grandmother died. I don't reckon _____.

2 I suppose it's possible that she'll succeed, but I don't believe _____.

3 I guess she might be under 50, but I don't suppose _____.

4 I guess it's just possible she loves him, but I don't imagine _____.

5 The irritating thing is, she's incredibly thin and yet I don't think _____.

6 I know so much about her and yet I don't suppose _____.

Exercise 3

Put each sentence into the correct order.

1 predict he / won't / I / the / win / . / election

_____

2 bet he / even / remember / I / me / . / won't

_____

3 assume you / heard / the / I / news / . / haven't

_____

4 hope the / . / I / doesn't / crash / market / sincerely

_____

5 presume they / left / I / yet / haven't / .

_____

6 suspect they / . / don't / much / I / have / money

_____

Exercise 4

Which sentences are correct?

1 I don't guess you'll be going to the party tonight, as Jess is ill. ❑

2 I don't assume you know what's happened. ❑

3 I bet she won't even notice me. ❑

4 I guess you won't be going away this summer. ❑

5 I suspect Kelly won't be fit enough to compete. ❑

6 I really don't hope the euro collapses. ❑

Exercise 5

Choose the correct word.

1 I don't **guess / assume / suppose** you saw Kerry on your travels?

2 To be honest, I don't **think / predict / bet** she'll make it as an actress.

3 She doesn't **suspect / expect / presume** she'll see him again.

4 We don't **imagine / predict / guess** they'll be coming to visit any time soon.

5 I just don't **suspect / believe / assume** he has the drive to succeed.

Exercise 6

Write the missing words in sentence B so that it means the same as sentence A.

1 **A** I don't imagine she'll want to go.
  B I suspect _____.

2 **A** I guess he can't be more than 30.
  B I don't reckon _____.

3 **A** I assume Clare hasn't spoken to her manager.
  B I don't expect _____.

4 **A** I don't suppose they'll visit us again.
  B I assume _____.

17

Passives (1)

Using passives when the active verb has two objects

be + -ed participle

In this unit you learn to use alternative passives from active verbs having two objects.

When you use a passive form of a verb with two objects such as **send**, **pay**, **buy**, **give**, **teach** and **show**, either the direct object or the indirect object can become the subject. For example, instead of *The firm paid the sales staff a bonus*, you can say *A bonus **was paid** to the sales staff*, where the direct object of the active clause (*the bonus*) is the subject of the passive clause.

The indirect object (*sales staff*) can be mentioned after **to** or **for**.

Sometimes it is unnecessary to mention the indirect object at all.

> *A bonus **was paid** at the end of the year.*

But you can also say *The sales staff **were paid** a bonus*, where the indirect object of the active clause is the subject of the passive clause.

> *I'm sure the letter **was sent** to Laura.*
> *The dog **was bought** for him as a birthday present.*
> *The children do not speak Gaelic at home, though they **are taught** it in school.*

*He **was shown** a photocopy of the certificate.*
*I **was given** this necklace by my grandmother.*

Remember!

There are some verbs that can have two objects but can only have one passive form. For example, you can say *They explained the situation to the manager*. However, there is only one possible passive, one that starts with the direct object, *The situation **was explained** to the manager*. You cannot say ~~The manager was explained the situation~~.

Verbs such as **want**, **demonstrate**, **exclude**, **emphasize**, **deliver** behave in the same way.

Exercise 1

Write the missing words in sentence B so that it means the same as sentence A.

1 A The letter was shown to the police.
  B The police _____.

2 A The leftovers were fed to the chickens.
  B The chickens _____.

3 A His wife was given his medals.
  B His medals _____.

4 A Several prizes were awarded to her for her work.
  B She _____ for her work.

5 A Everything he wanted was bought for him.
  B He _____ he wanted.

6 A Half an hour was allocated to us for our presentation.
  B We _____ for our presentation.

Exercise 2

Write the correct passive form of the verb in brackets to complete each sentence, as shown.

1 The prize will __*be awarded*__ (award) to the team with the most correct answers.

2 It _____ (announce) yesterday that the couple are to divorce.

3 She claimed that the money _____ (give) to her by an admirer.

4 We _____ (show) great courtesy by our hosts.

5 After several phone calls, a place on another flight _____ (find) for Martha so she was able to attend the meeting.

6 More than £50,000 a year _____ (pay) to outside consultants.

Exercise 3

Choose the correct words or phrases.

1 He was given his job back when **his employer was proved / it was proved to his employer** that he had not committed fraud.

2 A bonus **will be paid to all staff / will be paid all staff** at the end of the year.

3 They were happier once **they were explained the safety measures / the safety measures were explained to them**.

4 **All his children / For all his children** were bought their own apartments.

5 The documents **were sent / were sent to** his lawyer.

6 **We were reported the findings / The findings were reported to us** before they were published in the press.

Exercise 4

Put each sentence into the correct order.

1 allocated / at the back / We were / . / of the building / an office

_____

2 explained to us / were not / . / It was / that the tickets / refundable

_____

3 the audience that / . / was sick / announced to / the lead actor / It was

_____

4 She was sent a letter / had been excluded / that her daughter / to tell her / by the school / .

_____

5 special passes / were given / the conference hall / The journalists / . / to allow them into

_____

6 a grant / over a wider area / The charity / . / to extend its services / has been awarded

_____

Exercise 5

Complete the sentences by writing one word in each gap.

| fed | demonstrated | awarded | played | reported | poured |

1 Samir was _____ a scholarship to a prestigious music school.

2 The importance of staying within the law was _____ to us by Michael's problems.

3 We were _____ a recording of his speech.

4 Max was _____ a large glass of water by his brother.

5 His trial was _____ on national TV.

6 The prisoners were _____ a diet of bread and water.

Exercise 6

Are the highlighted words correct or incorrect in the sentences?

1 **To me was guaranteed** ❑ a job when I came out of the army.

2 A petition opposing the building of a new airport was delivered **to the prime minister** ❑.

3 **To all staff** ❑ will be sent a copy of the report.

4 His family **were not told** ❑ the cause of his death.

5 When he arrived at the house, he **was refused entry** ❑ by a bodyguard.

6 A valuable necklace **was lent the princess** ❑ by an admirer.

Exercise 7

Which sentences are correct?

1 Participants were each given a map and a set of instructions. ❑

2 They were emphasized that the area can be dangerous in bad weather. ❑

3 Thankfully, he was found some dry clothes by his teacher. ❑

4 A letter was sent Mr Jones, explaining the changes to the contract. ❑

5 Hannah was told the infection had spread to her lungs. ❑

6 The children were explained how to set up the experiment. ❑

Exercise 8

Decide if the pairs of sentences have the same meaning.

1 **A** No interviews were given to the press.
   B The press were not given any interviews. ❑

2 **A** He was told that there were things that he could do about his condition and was taught relaxation exercises.
   B He was told that there were things that he could do about his condition with relaxation exercises. ❑

3 **A** No one on the board of directors was paid a bonus for the last financial year.
   B A bonus was not paid to some people on the board of directors for the last financial year. ❑

4 **A** A photograph of Sven was shown to all the children in the school.
   B All the children in the school were photographed with Sven. ❑

5 **A** All members of the club were sent a postal questionnaire.
   B A questionnaire was sent through the post to all members of the club. ❑

6 **A** The car was bought for Erika by her husband.
   B Erika was bought the car by her husband. ❑

Exercise 9

For each sentence, tick the correct ending.

1 The trophy
   ❑ will be presented to the winning gymnast at the end of the tournament.
   ❑ will present to the winning gymnast at the end of the tournament.

2 They make such a fuss of their dog and
   ❑ the finest beef steak is only fed to him.
   ❑ he is only fed the finest beef steak.

3 All the main curriculum subjects
   ❑ are taught on the course.
   ❑ are having been taught on the course.

4 End of year reports
   ❑ will be sent home to your parents.
   ❑ will be shown home to your parents.

5 The document was highly confidential, and
   ❑ the need for secrecy was emphasized to all staff.
   ❑ all staff were emphasized the need for secrecy.

6 Olga was sad to lose her watch as
   ❑ it had been given to her by Ben.
   ❑ Ben had been given it by her.

18

Passives (2)
Using passive *-ing* and *to* forms

be + -ed participle
be + being + -ed participle
-ing form + -ed participle

In this unit you learn to use passives formed by **be** + *-ed* participle, **be** + **being** + *-ed* participle or *-ing* form + *-ed* participle.

Passive infinitive
The ordinary passive infinitive consists of **to be**, followed by the *-ed* participle.

> They opted **to be flown** home the next day.
> We need these clothes **to be cleaned** by Friday.
> There was nothing **to be done** for the unfortunate animal.
> She appears **to have been totally forgotten**.
> Women seem **to be being promoted** more often than in the past.

Here are the passive infinitives. The passive infinitives marked with a star are very rarely used.

to be eaten

to be being eaten*

to have been eaten

to have been being eaten*

Passive *-ing* forms
The ordinary passive *-ing* form consists of **being** and the *-ed* participle.

> I object to **being asked** to do it.
> **Being told to do** something one doesn't want to do is awful.
> **Having been declared** fit, he was allowed to leave the hospital.
> They were taken to the airport after **having been issued** with visas.

Here are the passive *-ing* forms. The *-ing* form marked with a star is very rarely used.

being eaten

having been eaten

having been being eaten*

Exercise 1

Match the sentence halves.

1	The princess prefers not	**a**	being stared at.
2	Most people hate	**b**	to be treated differently from everyone else.
3	Lisa often imagines her life	**c**	to be given to charity.
4	The millionaire wants most of his money	**d**	being changed by a win on the lottery.
5	The poet dreamt about his poems	**e**	being accepted by a leading publisher.

Exercise 2

Choose the correct word or words.

1 Few problems were caused by the baby **to be / being** born a month early.

2 The staff expect **to be / being** paid on Wednesday.

3 I'm interested in **to be / being** taught to sing.

4 Are all these people waiting **to be / being** seen by Dr Ronalds?

5 The cherry cakes from that shop are said **to be / being** the best in the North.

6 The team are hoping **to be / being** awarded a national prize for design this year.

Exercise 3

Complete the sentences by writing one word in each gap.

| being | making | served | said | mind | told |

1 When would you like dinner to be _____?

2 The children were enjoying themselves so much that they forgot about _____ given jobs by their parents.

3 There is nothing to be _____ that can help them.

4 The police ought to be _____ about the accident.

5 Did you _____ being mistaken for your sister?

Exercise 4

Decide if the pairs of sentences have the same meaning.

1 **A** Being given so much money was not necessarily a good thing for Mark.
   B It was not necessarily good for Mark to be given so much money. ☐

2 **A** Lars needs his employment history to be checked before he gets offered the job.
   B Lars should ensure that he has the right employment history before he can go for the job. ☐

3 **A** Is the chicken ready to be taken out of the oven?
   B Is it time to take the chicken out of the oven? ☐

4 **A** The Earth was once believed to be flat.
   B People used to believe the Earth was flat. ☐

5 **A** Jack and Sita enjoyed being shown the place where celebrities got married.
   B Jack and Sita enjoyed showing celebrities where they got married. ☐

Exercise 5

Which sentences are correct?

1 Rita allowed her daughter to be taken sailing across the lake. ☐

2 The zoo is getting ready being inspected by an animal welfare organization. ☐

3 How did you be managed to award three free tickets? ☐

4 I refuse to be told what to do by a four-year-old! ☐

5 The tickets to see the band had to give to someone else because I was ill. ☐

6 The building began to be seeing as a masterpiece as soon as it was finished. ☐

Exercise 6

Find the wrong or extra word in each sentence.

1 The bones are being thought to be from a meat-eating dinosaur.

2 He put a helmet on because he didn't want to be hit himself by a falling rock.

3 I didn't mean what I said to be taken there seriously.

4 Being me chosen to play in the match was a big surprise.

5 Does your son remember being put him to bed last night?

6 Putting the lid on the pan prevents the rice for drying out.

Exercise 7

For each sentence, tick the correct ending.

1 The district
   ☐ is said to have been named after Christopher Columbus.
   ☐ is said to having been named after Christopher Columbus.

2 Pierre resented
   ☐ to be spoken to like a naughty child.
   ☐ being spoken to like a naughty child.

3 Time is running out, and
   ☐ something has to be done soon.
   ☐ something has to be doing soon.

4 The 16 crew are believed to be safe
   ☐ after to have been rescued by emergency services.
   ☐ after having been rescued by emergency services.

5 At school, Arabella chooses
   ☐ to be known as Bella.
   ☐ being known as Bella.

6 As Javier turned the corner,
   ☐ he noticed that he was being followed.
   ☐ he noticed that he has been followed.

19

Future perfect
Making predictions about the future

> *will / should* + **have** + *-ed* participle
>
> *will / should* + **have been** + *-ing* participle

In this unit you learn to use the future perfect and the future perfect continuous for prediction of the present or future.

By the end of the year, I **will have won** the junior championships. When I finish high school, I **will have been training** on my own for a long time but by the time I'm twenty I **will have started** training with a professional coach – and by the time I'm thirty I **will have got** a gold medal at the Olympic Games!

Future perfect

The future perfect is formed by using **will** or **shall**, followed by **have** and the *-ed* participle of the main verb. You can use it to talk about something that has not happened yet but will happen before a particular time in the future.

*Even after a year, they **won't have forgotten** you.*
*By next week we **will have reached** the end of the project.*
*By that time, I **shall have left** the country.*
*The children **won't have tidied up** before they left.*

> ### *Remember!*
> You must indicate the specific future time referred to by using a time adverbial or another clause.

This structure can also be used to make predictions or assumptions about the present time.

*As you **will have noticed**, there are no ashtrays.*
*She **will have found** my note by now.*
*By the middle of June all my new furniture **will have arrived**.*

Future perfect continuous

If you want to indicate the duration of an event at a specific time in the future, you can use the future perfect continuous.

*By the time the year ends, I **will have been living** here for eighteen months.*
*How long **will you have been studying** Greek when you finish this course?*
*At Christmas, Ana **will have been working** at the company for a year.*

> ### *Remember!*
> You need to use a time adverbial to indicate the future time and an adverbial of duration to state how long the event will last.

Exercise 1

Choose the correct word or words.

1 By the time we get to the party, all the food will **go / have gone**, won't it?

2 When they see Leon's haircut, they'll **get / have got** a shock!

3 Let's have the party on the 25th – we'll **do / have done** our exams by then.

4 Your parents will already **meet / have met** Mr Gibbs at your school, is that right?

5 Jenny will **tell / have told** us her news when she gets here.

Exercise 2

Put each sentence into the correct order.

1 arrived / will / have / ? / Katya / yet, / she / won't

_____

2 won't / have / They / the house / to clean / had / properly yet. / time

_____

3 mind by / will / . / tomorrow / change / Helen / her

_____

4 for 60 years next / been / My grandparents / have / . / married / August / will

_____

5 I presume. / told / about / Chris's / won't / promotion yet, / Lucia / have / been

_____

6 midday? / finished / runners / will / How many / have / by

_____

Exercise 3

Complete the sentences by writing one word in each gap.

| realized | married | seen | marrying | been | before | by |

1 The car will have been repaired _____ the time Paddy finishes work.

2 Their wedding was in 1990, so in 2020 they will have been _____ for 30 years.

3 Do you think the postman will have delivered my birthday cards _____ I go to school tomorrow?

4 How long will you have _____ waiting if the bus doesn't come until 6.30?

5 Paola won't have _____ that the play is starting early – shall we phone her?

6 I bet they won't have looked on the table so they won't have _____ our note.

Exercise 4

Are the highlighted words correct or incorrect in the sentences?

1 He'll have been **teaching** ❏ at this school for six years by this time next month.

2 When I take my Spanish exams in May, I'll only have been **studied** ❏ it for three months.

3 Kitty will have left school by the time Robbie **starts** ❏.

4 I know Giuseppe **won't have** ❏ washed up. He never does!

5 When we've painted this room, we **will have done** ❏ the whole house.

6 The train leaves in an hour – **have you finished** ❏ packing by then?

Exercise 5

Find the wrong or extra word in each sentence.

1 The train will have left by the time we shall get to the station.

2 I'm going into town on Saturday, but the jeans I want will probably have being sold out by then.

3 When the Smiths will leave tomorrow evening, we'll have had a whole weekend of their complaining!

4 The restaurant will have close before we get there if you don't hurry up.

5 Don't worry, that noise will only have been made my brother's motorbike.

6 The rain is forecast to carry on until Tuesday, by which time it will have been caused the river to overflow its banks.

Exercise 6

Write the correct form of the verb in brackets to complete each sentence.

1 We'll be at the cinema in half an hour – will the film _____ (start) by then?

2 Do you think the baby will have _____ (go to sleep) by the time I come home?

3 My mum will have texted me a hundred times before the plane's even _____ (leave) the airport!

4 I think my phone battery will have _____ (run out) long before I arrive at the hostel.

5 I will have been _____ (write) for the college magazine longer than anyone else by the end of the year.

6 I _____ (not think) those guests will have understood a word the receptionist said.

20

Should and the subjunctive
Using reported clauses with and without modals

In this unit you learn to use **should** in an object clause. You also learn that when you leave out the modal you form the subjunctive.

Submitting assignments

It is imperative that assignments be handed in on or before their due date. We **request that students inform** their course tutors as soon as they realize that their deadline will not be met. **That students agree** on a new due date with the tutor is also a requirement. When assignments are submitted late, marks will be deducted from the score awarded for the work, according to how late they are. So **it is clearly vital that students make** every effort to meet their submission deadlines.

It is strongly advised that students read very carefully the rules and guidelines given to them at the beginning of their course.

Remember!

- Students should hand in their assignments on or before the due date.

- Students should inform their course tutors that the deadline will not be met.

- Students should agree on a new date with the tutor.

- Students should make every effort to meet the deadline.

- Students should read the rules and guidelines carefully.

Should

When someone makes a suggestion about what someone else should do, you report it by using a **that**-*clause*. In British English, this clause often contains a modal, usually **should**.

*They recommended **that the proposal should be accepted**.*

The subjunctive

When you leave out the modal, the verb in the reported clause still has the form it would have if the modal were present. This verb form is called the subjunctive.

*They recommended **that the proposal be accepted**.*
*It was his doctor who advised **that he change his job**.*
*I suggested **that he bring them all to the party**.*
*He insists **that the regulations be followed**.*

It + be + important, etc., *that* + subjunctive

You can also say that something is important or necessary by using a sentence beginning with the impersonal pronoun **it**, followed by **is**, an adjective such as **important** and a **that**-*clause*. As above, you can leave in the modal, or remove it to form the subjunctive.

***It is essential that** the minister (should) be informed immediately.*
***It is vital that** you (should) know precisely what's happening.*

Exercise 1

Complete the sentences by writing one word in each gap.

pay | should | asked | get | train | be | join

1 We decided it was vital that we should _____ a good night's sleep before our journey.

2 Is it really necessary that Bill _____ so hard?

3 Dave _____ that I sing a few songs at the concert.

4 They've proposed that the footpath _____ be closed while work is carried out on it.

5 Jackson has suggested that I _____ his band.

6 When we broke his car window, the man next door demanded that we _____ for it immediately.

Exercise 2

Decide if the pairs of sentences have the same meaning.

1 A The band leader suggested the guitarist play faster.
  B The band leader always wants the guitarist to play louder. ☐

2 A Anja insisted on me being the one who went to the show.
  B Anja insisted that I should be the one to go to the show. ☐

3 A How much hay did Eleanor ask that we give each horse?
  B How much hay did Eleanor tell us to give each horse? ☐

4 A It is essential that we be united in our approach to the problem.
  B We must solve all our problems at once. ☐

5 A It's most important that an injured person stay warm.
  B Most importantly, an injured person must stay warm. ☐

Exercise 3

Match the sentence halves.

1 It is essential that the area in front of the school entrance always
2 The teachers are insisting that the school tie
3 It is not desirable that pupils
4 Some of the children have requested that their homework load
5 It has been proposed that some of the school playing fields

a be sold to raise funds.
b be reduced.
c be kept clear.
d be worn.
e be driven to school.

Exercise 4

Write the simple past form of the verb in brackets to complete each sentence.

1 Would you recommend that jackets be _____ (wear) for the trip?
2 It _____ (be) absolutely vital that you listen carefully to these instructions now.
3 How much food do you suggest that we _____ (take)?
4 Group leaders have requested that you _____ (leave) expensive gadgets at home.
5 Some of the parents suggested they should _____ (accompany) their children.
6 It _____ (be) necessary that we book the bus for the trip last June, to ensure we got the right vehicle.

Exercise 5

Find the wrong or extra word in each sentence.

1 Who on earth suggested the canteen to be painted bright purple?
2 It is vital that everyone should be understand the safety procedure.
3 It's not essential that *all* employees approve it the new design, as long as most do!
4 My friends recommended us that we should eat in the Greengate Café.
5 Can I just ask for that the cat be well looked after while we're away?
6 It is vital that Tilly must see the doctor as soon as possible.

Avoiding repetition by omitting *to*-infinitives

In this unit you learn to avoid repetition of the main verb by omitting the **to-infinitive** (with or without the need to retain the *to*).

| To: Julia |
| From: Ella |
| Subject: James |

Hi Julia

Good to hear from you!

You asked after James. Actually, I don't see as much of him as I'd like **to**. (Mind you, I'm to blame – I was supposed to call him last night and completely **forgot**!) I think he's happy – he certainly deserves **to be**. Such a lovely guy.

Don't know about you but I need a holiday. I'd fly off somewhere hot tomorrow if I could afford **to**. I hate my job. I'd resign if I dared **to**, but then I'd have even less money.

Anyway, I've got some work to do before bedtime, if I can bear **to**, that is. Very dull!

I'll call tomorrow for a chat.

Much love
Ella

In order to avoid repetition, you can leave words out of **to**-*infinitive* clauses. Instead of using a full **to**-*infinitive* clause after a verb, you can just use **to** if the action or state has already been mentioned. Instead of *He failed his exam but I don't think he deserved* **to fail it**, you can say:

He failed his exam but I don't think he deserved **to**.

Remember!

You can also do this in conversation to avoid repeating what the other person has said.

A *Do you ever visit a doctor?*

B *No. We can't afford* **to**.

There are some verbs, such as **try**, **want**, **forget**, **like**, **wish** and **ask**, that are also often used on their own, without **to**.

*I'm sure she'll see you, if you **ask**.*
*I'm going for a walk – you can come if you **want**.*
*I meant to call you but I **forgot**.*
*Please help yourself to whatever you'd **like** for breakfast.*

> ## Remember!
>
> The exception is the verb **to be** which has to be repeated.
> *The students were all at the station in good time as we had asked them **to be**.*

Exercise 1

Match the sentence halves.

1 I'd absolutely love to go skiing this year,
2 I'd certainly cut down on the fat in my diet
3 We could meet a bit earlier – say 6 o'clock,
4 The dining and reception rooms were all set out
5 He didn't win,
6 These days, I don't get to play as much tennis

a exactly as we had asked them to be.
b but he certainly deserved to.
c if the doctor said I had to.
d as I'd like to.
e if you could bear to.
f if only I could afford to.

Exercise 2

Put the correct word in each gap.

struggle | manage | hesitate | decide | mean | failed

Hi Eva

I was supposed to call you this evening but again [1]_____ to. Sorry! Here's a quick message before bedtime. Another hectic weekend – Ian's party Saturday night. I meant to leave at midnight, but didn't quite [2]_____ to (3:30 in the end!). I'm supposed to be going out four nights in a row this week, but, feeling like this, I think I'll [3]_____ to. I might cancel tomorrow night.

By the way, I haven't invited Paula to my party (yet). I'm thinking of it, but [4]_____ to in case Mike comes (they really don't get on!). I may still invite her – will let you know if I [5]_____ to.

Also, if I upset you last week with what I said about Peter, I really didn't [6]_____ to. I can be a bit blunt, I know. I'm sorry.

Right, bedtime!

Love

Poppy

Exercise 3

Complete the sentences by writing one word in each gap.

| mean | deserve | appeared | requested | afford | expected |

1 They won the championship, but they didn't _____ to. They certainly weren't the best team.

2 She offended Tanja with the remark, but I'm sure she didn't _____ to. It was definitely unintentional.

3 A lot of women only married at that young age because they were _____ to by society.

4 I'd buy a second home myself if I could _____ to.

5 The parcels were sent to the Beech Street address, exactly as I'd _____ them to be.

6 I think Hannah was happy, or at least she _____ to be. She was smiling most of the evening.

Exercise 4

Put each sentence into the correct order.

1 intended / him but / I / forgot / . / to email

_____

2 tonight if / I'll / to / I'm allowed / . / come out

_____

3 join us / tonight if he / He can / chooses to / . / for dinner

_____

4 my / I / I'd leave / dared to / . / job if

_____

5 sell the / had to / we / . / house if / We could

_____

6 now if / you / wish to / can pay / . / You

_____

Exercise 5

Which sentences are correct?

1 Ollie was really told off by the teacher, but I don't think he deserved to. ❑

2 Lena was smartly dressed for the wedding as I'd asked her to. ❑

3 I'm going to call in on Annie. Come along if you want. ❑

4 You can leave your luggage here if you wish. ❑

5 Flowers were displayed on all four tables, as we had requested them to be. ❑

6 I ended up buying far more food than I had planned to. ❑

Exercise 6

For each sentence, tick the correct ending.

1 Pilar doesn't have to go to the party
   - ☐ if she doesn't want to.
   - ☐ if she doesn't want.

2 Dan can easily score top marks in the test
   - ☐ if he tries to do.
   - ☐ if he tries.

3 You can come to my house before the party
   - ☐ if you like.
   - ☐ if you like to come.

4 Samir has hurt Hazel's feelings,
   - ☐ but he didn't intend.
   - ☐ but he didn't intend to.

5 The children were all outside with their coats on
   - ☐ as I had told them.
   - ☐ as I had told them to be.

6 Katya dressed in a suit for her interview
   - ☐ because she was expected to.
   - ☐ because she was expected.

Exercise 7

Decide if the pairs of sentences have the same meaning.

1 **A** David trod on Lisa's foot, but he didn't mean to.
  B David trod on Lisa's foot, but he didn't intend to. ☐

2 **A** Please leave the key under the doormat when you go out if you remember.
  B Please leave the key under the doormat if you remember to go out. ☐

3 **A** Julio tried to fix the model using glue, but didn't manage to.
  B Julio tried to fix the model using glue, but didn't succeed. ☐

4 **A** You can have a piece of cake if you ask nicely.
  B You can have a piece of cake if you ask to have it nicely. ☐

5 **A** Felix wasn't going to go to the meeting, but then, at the last minute, he decided to.
  B Felix wasn't going to go to the meeting, but then, at the last minute, he changed ☐
     his mind.

6 **A** Parents may attend the exhibition to view their children's work if they wish.
  B Parents may attend the exhibition to view their children's work if they want to do this. ☐

22

Politeness

Using past forms and *wonder* and *hope* to express politeness

In this unit you learn to use past tenses to express tentative politeness, especially with the verbs **hope** and **wonder**.

Using past tenses to show politeness is a common feature of functional English. For example *Could I have a glass of water?* is more polite than *Can I have a glass of water?* Other polite forms include:

> *Was there something you wanted?*
> *Did you have a question?*
> *Were you looking for a particular kind of shoe?*

Using the reporting verbs **hope** and **wonder** in the past tense is another way of being polite.

> *I was hoping you could help me.*
> *We hoped that you'd be able to take us to the airport this evening.*
> *I wondered if we might be allowed to look around now?*
> *I was wondering whether you had this in size 18?*

> ### Remember!
> **Wonder** is not followed by **if** or **whether** when it comes at the end of the sentence:
> *Could we have a piece of cake now, I was wondering?*

Exercise 1

Match the sentence halves.

1 I wondered	**a** you could give Simon a lift.
2 I was hoping	**b** Simon getting a lift with you?
3 Were you planning	**c** give Simon a lift?
4 Did you think you could	**d** might give Simon a lift?
5 Was there a possibility that you	**e** to give Simon a lift?
6 Is there any chance of	**f** if you would mind giving Simon a lift?

Exercise 2

Put each sentence into the correct order.

1 borrow / I / hoping / was / to / car tonight / . / your

_____

2 of / were / you / jacket / looking / What / ? / for / kind

_____

3 there / ? / an / Was / particularly liked / you / author

_____

4 if / ? / were / wondering / donation / you could / us / We / a / give

_____

5 to / I / ask / if / wanted / be / could / turned down / . / the heating

_____

6 me / , / you / ? / did / Excuse / want / something

_____

Exercise 3

Choose the correct word.

1 I was **hoping / wondering / expecting** if you could help me.
2 I wondered if I **might / am / said** ask you a question?
3 **Was / Could / Might** there something I can help you with?
4 We were **hoping / wondering / asking** you could help us.
5 I **hoping / will hope / hoped** you might be able to lend me some money.

Exercise 4

Write the missing words in sentence B so that it means the same as sentence A.

1 **A** Would it be possible for me to leave my bag with you and collect it later?

   B I was _____ if I could leave my bag with you and collect it later.

2 **A** Did you want a double or a single room, madam?

   B _____ you like a double or a single room, madam?

3 **A** What kind of suitcase did you want, sir?

   B What kind of suitcase were you _____ for, sir?

4 **A** Do you think you could repair this watch?

   B I was _____ that you could repair this watch.

Exercise 5

Decide if the pairs of sentences have the same meaning.

1 **A** I was planning to come and see you later.
   B I am thinking about coming to see you later. ❑

2 **A** Which of these cakes did you want?
   B What kind of cakes did you use to like? ❑

3 **A** I'd like to get tickets for the show at 7 p.m.
   B I was hoping to get tickets for the show at 7 p.m. ❑

4 **A** We were wondering if you'd like to come with us.
   B We thought about asking you to come with us. ❑

5 **A** Was it the chocolate or the strawberry ice cream that you wanted?
   B Would you like the strawberry or the chocolate ice cream? ❑

Exercise 6

Which sentences are correct?

1 We were wondering you could help us? ❑

2 We hoped you wouldn't mind wait for us. ❑

3 How many large envelopes did you need? ❑

4 I hope you could post this letter for me. ❑

5 Were you trying to find the exit? ❑

6 I just wanted to ask you if you could move your car – it's blocking the road. ❑

Exercise 7

Complete the sentences by writing one word in each gap.

1 I was _____ if I could have another cup of coffee?

2 Would it be possible to book the hall for tomorrow, we _____ wondering?

3 I just wanted to _____ you a question.

4 Was _____ a refund or a credit note that you wanted?

5 We wondered _____ we might come and visit you later?

6 Were _____ any problems that I could help you with?

23

Sentence connectors and conjunctions

In this unit you learn to use conjunctions between clauses in a sentence and connectors between sentences. This helps you to form coherent texts when you write or speak.

Connections between clauses in a sentence

When you put two clauses into one sentence, you use a conjunction to link them and to show the relationship between them.

> They went by bus **because** it was cheap.
> The cake looked wonderful, **but** it was too dry to eat.
> Jalila had learnt to cook **in order that** her mother could have a day off sometimes.
> Her sister told her nothing about it, **except that** the event had taken place.
> He put the book back in place **just as** it had been.

You can use one of the following conjunctions:

Connections between clauses in a sentence

Coordinating conjunctions	and but or
Conjunctions used in purpose clauses	in order that so as to so that
Conjunctions used in reason clauses	because in case since
Conjunctions used in concessive clauses	although despite even if except that not that whereas while
Conjunctions used in clauses of manner	as like just as

Connections between sentences

You use sentence connectors to show what sort of connection there is between one sentence and another.

*We arrived early. **However**, the bus had already left.*
*Taxis were provided for the delegates. **Therefore**, the rain was not an issue.*
*She struggled with the problem of gaining weight. **Furthermore**, there was no advice that helped.*
*'You are what you eat' does have some truth to it. **By the same token**, before we are born, we are what our mothers eat.*
*She didn't know how long he might be. **In the meantime**, she could only sit there waiting.*

You can introduce a related comment or an extra reinforcing piece of information using one of the following connectors:

Connections between sentences

To compare with something already mentioned	also as well furthermore moreover
To add a fact that illustrates the same point as the one you have just made, or a suggestion that has the same basis	again by the same token equally likewise
To contrast with the previous sentence or give another point of view	alternatively by contrast conversely even so however nevertheless on the contrary on the other hand rather then again
To say that the fact you are mentioning exists because of the fact or facts previously given	accordingly as a result consequently hence therefore
To indicate that something takes place after or before an event that you have already mentioned or at the same time as that event	at the same time beforehand finally in the meantime later meanwhile next previously simultaneously soon subsequently throughout

Exercise 1

Are the highlighted words correct or incorrect in this text?

Adam was going to be speaking to you this morning, but unfortunately he's unable to be here. [1]**Consequently** ❑, I've been asked to say a few words about the launch of this product. [2]**However** ❑, before I start I'd like to look back, for a moment, on the last two years. I think we'd all agree it's been a challenging undertaking and we've encountered our fair share of problems. [3]**Hence** ❑, it's been exhausting and, at times, frustrating. [4]**Furthermore** ❑, it's been extremely enjoyable and rewarding. [5]**Furthermore** ❑, I think we've all learned a lot along the way. [6]**Therefore** ❑ I think we can all be very proud of ourselves and proud of the product that we've jointly created.

Exercise 2

Rearrange the letters to find words. Use the definitions to help you.

1 rofherete _____ (used to introduce a logical result or conclusion)

2 whemanile _____ (while a particular thing is happening)

3 heewras _____ (used to introduce a comment which contrasts with what is said in the main clause)

4 ewohrev _____ (used when you are adding a comment which is surprising or which contrasts with what has just been said)

5 yb snortact _____ (used to show that you are now mentioning a very different situation from the one you have just mentioned)

6 venretehsels _____ (used when saying something that contrasts with what has just been said)

Exercise 3

For each sentence, tick the correct ending.

1 I have two dresses in my wardrobe whereas
   ❑ my sister has 23.
   ❑ I need a couple more.

2 We had a tiny house and very little money. Nevertheless,
   ❑ we were quite dissatisfied with our lives.
   ❑ we were perfectly content with our lives.

3 We had our health and enough money to live on. Furthermore,
   ❑ it wasn't enough.
   ❑ we had each other.

4 I had spent all but $50 of my budget. Consequently,
   ❑ I was living on a meagre diet of bread and water.
   ❑ I was still having a marvellous time.

5 There is a limited supply of apartments on the campus. Therefore
   ❑ we are confident that we will be able to provide you with accommodation.
   ❑ we recommend that you apply for housing before the official deadline.

Exercise 4

Decide if the pairs of sentences have the same meaning.

1 **A** This is by no means an easy task. Nevertheless, we persevere, trusting that our efforts will be rewarded.
   B This is by no means an easy task, but we persevere, trusting that our efforts will be rewarded. ☐

2 **A** I spent a modest £30 on my trainers. By contrast, my husband spent £120 on his!
   B I spent a modest £30 on my trainers, whereas my husband spent £120 on his! ☐

3 **A** It was an exhausting trip and not without stress. Nevertheless, we found it useful and in parts, even enjoyable.
   B It was an exhausting trip and not without stress. However, we found it useful and in parts, even enjoyable. ☐

4 **A** We arrived at 9 o'clock. Consequently, the bus had already left.
   B We arrived at 9 o'clock but the bus had already left. ☐

Exercise 5

Which sentences are correct?

1 Our headquarters are currently being refurbished. Meanwhile, we're using the building opposite as a temporary office. ☐

2 The job isn't ideal in that I have to travel too much and the hours are long. However, it's not all bad. ☐

3 It's a lovely, spacious apartment and it's in a very nice part of town. Furthermore, it's very close to where I work. ☐

4 The company I work for are great actually, and my colleagues are first-rate. Nevertheless, I'd like to stay with them for a few years. ☐

5 No one was willing to give evidence in court. Accordingly, the case was dropped. ☐

6 Sara does a job share for 20 hours a week, whereas I do something very similar. ☐

Exercise 6

Choose the correct word or phrase.

1 I have a tiny, one-bedroom apartment in the city. **Meanwhile / Nevertheless / Therefore**, my sister has a huge house in the country.

2 I lived on my own. **Consequently / Hence / However**, I wasn't lonely.

3 He never went out and met anyone. **Consequently / By contrast / Nevertheless**, he didn't have any friends to speak of.

4 People generally admire Michael professionally. **Nevertheless / Therefore / Furthermore**, they like him as a person, and that's definitely more important.

5 She wasn't the most reliable of colleagues and her behaviour was quite erratic. **Furthermore / Nevertheless / Meanwhile**, she could be quite inspired and she was fun to work with.

24

Which, whose, how much and how many

Asking questions about things outside the main clause

In this unit you learn to use pushdown questions with **which**, **whose**, **how much** and **how many**.

In pushdown questions, the thing being questioned is not directly in the main clause, it is only part of an element, for example, part of the object, part of an adjunct or part of a subordinate clause.

If the main clause is *Mike caught measles*, then *Whose child did Mike catch measles from?* is a pushdown question because it questions part of the adjunct. However, *Who did Mike catch measles from?* is not a pushdown question because it questions the adjunct in the main clause.

If the main clause is *I bought presents for the children*, then *How many presents costing under £5 did you buy for the children?* is a pushdown question because it questions part of the adjunct that is not in the main clause. However, *How many presents did you buy for the children?* is not a pushdown question because it questions the adjunct in the main clause.

Examples of pushdown questions:

Which of our neighbours did you meet the son of?

This is a pushdown question because it does not question the main clause but a prepositional phrase that is part of the object. However, *Which of our neighbour's sons did you meet?* is not a pushdown question as it is questioning the main clause: *I met your neighbour's son.*

How much of the free time you had at the weekend did you spend watching TV?

This is a pushdown question because it questions part of the adjunct that is not in the main clause. However, *How much time did you spend watching TV?* is not a pushdown question as it is questioning the main clause: *I spent time watching TV.*

Examples that are not pushdown questions:

How much time do you need to finish your work?

This is not a pushdown question because it questions the object in the main clause: *You need some time.*

Exercise 1

Match the sentence halves.

1 Which aspect of the research

2 What was the precise point

3 What have the responses to the survey you carried out

4 Which figures did you say

5 Do you know the title of the journal

6 Where did your initial findings

a lead you to search for additional sources on the same subject?

b had to be discarded after you realized they were inaccurate?

c led you to expect with regard to likely future trends?

d do you consider most likely to present difficulties in writing up?

e at which you realized that your theory was untenable?

f in which the article you're looking for appeared?

Exercise 2

Complete the sentences by writing one phrase in each gap.

are you planning | will you ask | was the questionnaire | do researchers often find
do you think is used | need to be considered | do you consider it

1 How useful _____ to draft an outline of an essay before writing it?

2 Which system of providing source references _____ by the majority of researchers?

3 Which methods _____ the discussion group to use in order to provide feedback on your proposals?

4 Which section of your dissertation _____ to write up first?

5 What _____ prevents them from starting to write up their work?

6 What sample size _____ based on that provided the evidence you're using?

Exercise 3

Which sentences are correct?

1 Which type of cheese did you tell me you wanted to buy for the party? ❑

2 Whose father you said you went to university with? ❑

3 How long do you think should I wait for her to arrive? ❑

4 Which river did they say they tried to swim across? ❑

5 How many matches are you glad because the team won? ❑

6 Which file is the form that I need to complete in? ❑

Exercise 4

Are the highlighted words correct or incorrect in the sentences?

1 Who **should children under the age of 14 be accompanied by** ❑ if they want to see the film?

2 Who **you said offered to help us** ❑ if we got into any difficulty?

3 Whose children **should we not disturb** ❑?

4 Where **did you go where had you never been** ❑ before?

5 What **did John offer to help us by doing** ❑?

6 Which **car manufacturer has just withdrawn their latest model** ❑ from the market?

Exercise 5

Find the wrong or extra word in each sentence.

1 How large a percentage of people who buy this brand of washing powder are they in the top three socio-economic classes?

2 Which station did you say whether I should get off at?

3 How much more did Mario spend during his holiday than had he intended?

4 Who do you think Stefan saw him crossing the road outside the supermarket?

5 How long did he say if he was going to wait for?

6 What do you think we should ask that Daphne to bring to the meeting?

Exercise 6

Decide if the pairs of sentences have the same meaning.

1 **A** How many shoes costing under £20 do they sell in the shop?
   B How many shoes do they sell in the shop? ❑

2 **A** Whose book did you tell the teacher you had borrowed?
   B When you told the teacher you had borrowed a book, who did you say you ❑ borrowed it from?

3 **A** How much money did you say that her father earns in a year?
   B Tell me how much money her father earns in a year. ❑

4 **A** Which of the college rules is considered by you to be the most important?
   B Which of the college rules do you consider to be the most important? ❑

5 **A** Which shelf are the clothes that you're wearing to the party on?
   B Can you show me the shelf where the clothes that you're wearing to the party are? ❑

6 **A** Did you say how long Matthew is staying for?
   B How long did Matthew say that he would be staying for? ❑

Exercise 7

For each sentence, tick the correct ending.

1 The experiment was to see
   ❑ which sort of tree trapped the most air pollution.
   ❑ how much of the trees trapped the most air pollution.

2 Amelia asked him
   ❑ whose daughter he had taken her to the cinema.
   ❑ whose daughter he had taken to the cinema.

3 Which of the chairs
   ❑ did you make a cover for?
   ❑ made you a cover for?

4 How many of the apples that we picked at the weekend
   ❑ you put in the pies?
   ❑ did you put in the pies?

5 Nobody knew
   ❑ whose essay Michel had copied his from.
   ❑ whose essay did Michel copy his from.

6 How much of their worktime
   ❑ do staff spend speaking on the phone?
   ❑ do staff spend to speak on the phone?

25

Phrasal verbs (1)

Two-word phrasal and prepositional verbs

In this unit you learn to use two-word phrasal and prepositional verbs and the correct position of the object.

There is a special group of verbs formed of two or three words. These are called phrasal verbs. They consist of:

a verb followed by an adverb:

> They **sat down**.
> The music gradually **died away**.

a verb followed by a preposition (sometimes called a prepositional verb):

> She **looked after** her sick mother.
> She **fell down** the steps.
> Don't **count on** James.

> ### Remember!
>
> The nouns at the end of the examples above (*sick mother*, *the steps*, *James*) are objects of the prepositions and not direct objects of the verbs. Therefore the noun phrase always comes after the preposition, even when it is a pronoun.
>
> Don't **count on** him. NOT ~~Don't count him on~~.

When you are using a phrasal verb with an object that is a short noun phrase, you usually have a choice as to where you put the object. It can be placed either after the second word of the phrasal verb or after the first word and before the second word.

> He **filled up** his car with petrol.
> She **filled** my glass **up**.

When the object consists of a long noun phrase, it is more likely to come after the second word of the phrasal verb.

> Officials have been asked to **hold back** all documentation relating to the court case.
> He promised to **give away** five per cent of all of his future earnings to charity.
> I **knocked over** the table at the side of her bed as I walked past.

When the object is a pronoun it usually comes before the second word of the phrasal verb. This is because it is not new information, and so it is not put in a position of prominence at the end of the clause.

*I waited until he had **emptied it out**.*
*He **tied it up** and **threw it into** the car.*

If the object of a phrasal verb is an abstract noun such as **hope**, **confidence** or **support**, it usually comes after the second word of the phrasal verb.

*We are hoping to **build up confidence** in the company.*
*His opponent **put up a lot of resistance**.*
*She didn't **hold out much hope** for their return.*

With a small number of phrasal verbs, the object is always placed between the first and the second words of the verb. For example, you can say *I can't **tell your brothers apart*** but not *I can't tell apart your brothers*. Here are some more examples:

*The headmaster was **ordering everybody about**.*
*He **answered his father back**.*

Remember!

Some phrasal verbs have more than one transitive sense. For example, **take back** has the object between the first and the second word when it means *remind someone of something* but when it means *regain something* the object can come in between or at the end.

*The smell of the corridor **took the man back** to his schooldays.*
*The athlete's ambition of **taking back his world title** remained unfulfilled.*

Exercise 1

Are the highlighted words correct or incorrect in this text?

Hi Sammy

Thanks for your email – it was lovely to find your news from home when I [1]**switched on my computer** this morning.

I started my Swedish course on Monday, and so far it's been really good. There's a huge amount of new language [2]**for me to take in**, so I'm working hard after classes as well as at school. [3]**The course goes on** till 6 every evening, so it's quite intense! I feel like I'm [4]**picking them up** very slowly but that's probably because there's such a lot to learn. I've started writing my first assignment today and we've got to [5]**hand in** next Friday. I've made some great new friends, and we all [6]**hang us out** together when we have any free time.

Write again soon

Anita

Exercise 2

For each sentence, tick one or two correct endings.

1 This old car is always breaking
   - ❑ it down.
   - ❑ down.
   - ❑ itself down.
   - ❑ down the car.

2 I've dropped an earring under your chair – please can you pick
   - ❑ up it?
   - ❑ up my earring?
   - ❑ up?
   - ❑ it up?

3 I've decided to give
   - ❑ up all the things I do that get me down.
   - ❑ all up the things I do that get me down.
   - ❑ all the things I do that get me down up.
   - ❑ all the things that get me up down.

4 I need to watch what I eat because of all the weight I've recently put
   - ❑ on.
   - ❑ it on.
   - ❑ on it.
   - ❑ on to me.

5 Ferdinand has gone into town to look
   - ❑ a new bike for.
   - ❑ for a new bike.
   - ❑ it for a new bike.
   - ❑ for him a new bike.

Exercise 3

Put each sentence into the correct order.

1 come / you / and / Can / pick / from Lara's / ? / me / up

_____

2 not to / Please try / us / up / . / wake

_____

3 his / for / looking / . / phone / the café / in / Jacob's

_____

4 mustn't / give / in / You / to / ! / temptation

_____

5 Have / when / found / out / Rick / is / you / stay / coming / to / ?

_____

6 across / dance music / I've never before / type / come / this / of / .

_____

Exercise 4

Find the words or phrases that do not belong.

1 look it	up	at	for	over
2 fill in	him	this form	it	the gaps
3 take it	back	after	off	for
4 come	across it	back it	out it	off it

Exercise 5

Find the wrong or extra word in each sentence.

1 The concert organizers have decided to put it off concert until the singer has recovered.

2 Please go away you until I've finished my work.

3 I hope they never find out who it made the mistake.

4 My grandparents brought me and my brothers up them.

5 I know I can always count him on Tom.

6 She filled in writing the form very quickly.

Exercise 6

Match the two parts together.

1 I saw the bus leaving the stop and ran, but I couldn't catch   a it in.

2 I shared a flat with Tessa for a while but it didn't work   b off it.

3 I always liked fast food until a documentary put me   c out.

4 I tried to solve the puzzle but I couldn't work   d it off.

5 You must see the doctor soon – don't put   e it up.

6 I'd finished all my coursework but I forgot to hand   f it out.

26

Phrasal verbs (2)

Three-word phrasal and prepositional verbs

In this unit you learn to use three-word phrasal and prepositional verbs and the correct position of the object.

To: Alun
From: Laura
Subject: Meeting with Antonio

Hello Alun
I had a meeting with Antonio yesterday and he **let me in on** the deal. We are going to go to two other businesses and get them both to make us an offer. Then we are going to **play the two of them off against** each other. We'll take the highest bidder. It could be a tricky negotiation though and I'm not sure what I've **let myself in for**.

Regards
Laura

Some phrasal verbs consist of three words: a verb, an adverb and a preposition. This type of verb is sometimes called a phrasal-prepositional verb. Most three-word phrasal verbs are intransitive. The preposition at the end is followed by its own object.

> His girlfriend **walked out on** him.
> They **got away with** overcharging us for six months.
> How did you **put up with** it?

A few three-word phrasal verbs are transitive. The direct object of the verb comes immediately after the verb. A second noun phrase is put after the preposition, as normal.

> They tried to **turn us out of** our home.
> Bill tried to **talk them out of** it.
> Who **put you up to** this trick?

These are some transitive three-word phrasal verbs:

do out of	put down to
frighten out of	put up to
let in for	take out on
let in on	take up on
play off against	talk out of
put down as	turn out of

Exercise 1

Choose the correct words or phrases.

1 Nicola looks really well at the moment. I put **it down to / down to it** the fact she's changed her job.

2 I'm so disappointed that our holiday was cancelled. I was really **looking forward to a break / looking forward a break to**.

3 Martin argued with his girlfriend, but now he wants to make **her up with it / it up with her**.

4 Good teachers always look **students out for / out for students** who might be struggling to keep up.

5 Jim always stood **up for what he believed in / what he believed in up for** and people respected him for that.

Exercise 2

Put the correct word or words in each gap.

> up | him | back | you | his stuff | college | me

Hi Stef

Hope you found your bike lock key and you managed to get ¹_____ to your flat OK yesterday? It was great to catch ²_____ with everyone again after the holidays, especially Tom. He's so nice, I don't think anyone could ever fall out with ³_____! I'm glad he's decided not to drop out of ⁴_____. He's going to live in halls of residence this year and I've offered to help him move all ⁵_____ into the flat on Tuesday. If you're around then, it would be great if you could come and help ⁶_____ and Tom out with the move.

Are you in tonight? I could pop over to see you.

Bye for now

Ned

Exercise 3

Write the words in brackets in the correct order to complete each sentence.

1 Ahmet's a naughty little boy but he never gets caught. How does he get _____ (with it away)?

2 Let's meet, so I can catch _____ (up your news on).

3 The shop where Anthony worked closed, so that put _____ (of him out) a job.

4 Sara's lovely. You'd _____ (on get her with) really well, I think.

5 Was it Mohammed who put _____ (you to up) playing this trick on me?

6 You've bought so many tinned tomatoes that we won't _____ (out them run of) for about five years!

Exercise 4

Put each sentence into the correct order.

1 to / I / cut / need / I spend / down / of money / on / . / the amount

_____

2 with / Be / ! / you / off

_____

3 the broken vase / . / wrapped / She / up in / and / newspaper / away / it / threw

_____

4 with / it / on / ! / Get

_____

5 do / set / you / When / work / off / ? / for

_____

6 annoyed if / don't / you / along / . / go / with / He / his wishes / gets

_____

Exercise 5

Decide if the pairs of sentences have the same meaning.

1 **A** I'll look out for your glove while I'm cleaning. ☐
  B I'll look out your glove for you while I'm cleaning.

2 **A** I was brought up by my aunt and uncle. ☐
  B My aunt and uncle brought me up.

3 **A** Hannah turned up with a bunch of flowers for me. ☐
  B Hannah turned a bunch of flowers up at the door for me.

4 **A** Do you get along with all your brothers? ☐
  B Do you get all your brothers along with you?

5 **A** When it comes to cleaning, I definitely don't keep up to the same standard as my mum! ☐
  B I definitely don't keep my cleaning up to the same standard as my mum's.

Exercise 6

Which sentences are correct?

1 Ivan fell Nina out with, because she forgot his birthday! ☐

2 That watch was my dad's, so please take it good care of. ☐

3 It doesn't matter. Please put it out of your mind. ☐

4 Why were you turned away from the club? ☐

5 He and Marti had never got each other on well with. ☐

6 What did you get up to in Greece? ☐

27

Inversion (1)

Inversion after *so* + adjective, *such* + *be*, *neither* and *nor*

In this unit you learn to use structures that require inversion to give emphasis or show a shared negative between two parts of a sentence. Inversion means that you swap the normal position of the verb and the subject.

Inversion after *so* + adjective

You can use **so** to emphasize an adjective. For example, you can say *It's so cold today*. You can also put the **so** + *adjective* at the beginning of the sentence, but the verb and the subject must be inverted. You say:

*So well-funded **was the research** that results were achieved within months* NOT ~~So well funded the research was~~.

*So successful **were the kits** that the group's toy division soon became too big for the company to handle.*

*So angry **was he** with his father that Ben didn't talk to him for a few years.*

Inversion after *such* + *be*

If you want to emphasize a noun or noun phrase use **such** + **be**. Again, the subject and the verb *be* need to be inverted.

*Such **were the problems** at the airport that no planes took off for several hours.*

*Such **was her fear** that she refused to drive on the motorway.*

*Such **was the noise** that none of them heard David when he spoke again.*

*Such **were the pressures** of the business that Ines had to return to work three days later.*

Inversion after *neither* and *nor*

You also use inversion after **neither** and **nor** when you are saying that the previous negative statement also applies to another person or group.

*We aren't going to Spain this year, and **neither are the Watsons**.*

*I don't know where my phone is, **nor does anyone** else!*

*I've got nothing to lose, and **neither has Michelle**.*

*He himself isn't talking, and **nor are his lawyers**.*

Exercise 1

Choose the correct words.

1 I wasn't interested in history and neither **was Eva / Eva was**.

2 Our problems **were so great / so great were** that we had to give up the journey.

3 So splendid **was the palace / the palace was** that even the emperor was impressed.

4 My computer isn't working and nor **my phone is / is my phone**.

5 Such **was her dismay / her dismay was** at the news, I thought she might faint.

6 My brother **is such a liar / such a liar is** that I never know whether to believe him.

Exercise 2

Match the sentence halves.

1 We aren't going to Spain this year,

2 Such was the panic as we ran outside that

3 So relieved were his parents that

4 I've never been abroad,

5 Such was the awkwardness of the situation,

6 Kirsty didn't want to go skiing,

a I decided to make an excuse and leave.

b and neither are the Watsons.

c and nor has my wife.

d they forgot to reprimand him.

e and neither did I.

f I forgot to pick up my handbag.

Exercise 3

Complete the sentences by writing one word in each gap.

| overwhelming | arrogance | miserable | difficulty | restrictions | admired |

1 Such is his _____, he believes that nobody can beat him.

2 So _____ was she that she stayed in her room for a week.

3 Such were the _____ on our movements that we could rarely leave the city.

4 So _____ were her debts that they dominated her life.

5 Such was the _____ of contacting him that we spoke only three times in the year he was away.

6 So _____ are his paintings, people travel from distant countries to see them.

Exercise 4

Which sentences are correct?

1 I'm not intending to go to university and neither are most of my friends. ❑

2 So beautiful the girl was, everyone was staring at her. ❑

3 Barbara hasn't finished her essay and nor Kamal has. ❑

4 Such is the difficult to pass the exam, most students are not successful. ❑

5 So valuable were her jewels, they were kept in a special safe at night. ❑

6 Such was the greed of these people, they were prepared to cheat their own friends. ❑

Exercise 5

Put each sentence into the correct order.

1 bus fare / I couldn't / could Amy / . / afford the / and neither

_____

2 I should have done / far more than / that I ate / were the cakes / . / So delicious

_____

3 Such was / quite frightened / . / we were / the force of / his anger that

_____

4 the post office / . / isn't open / neither is / The bank / today and

_____

5 these soldiers / Such were the / that many of them / . / never recovered / dangers faced by

_____

6 that even his / his behaviour become / tired of him / So outrageous did / . / family grew

_____

Exercise 6

Write the missing words in sentence B so that it means the same as sentence A.

1 A The mountain was so high, we could not climb it in a day.

   B So _____, we could not climb it in a day.

2 A I didn't go to the concert and Jan didn't either.

   B I didn't go to the concert and neither _____.

3 A We felt so happy, we wanted to celebrate straight away.

   B Such _____ happiness that we wanted to celebrate straight away.

4 A Neither chemistry nor physics interests me much.

   B Chemistry doesn't interest me much and nor _____.

5 A The restaurant was so expensive, I barely had enough money to pay the bill.

   B So _____ that I barely had enough money to pay the bill.

6 A My brother and my father both hate opera.

   B My brother doesn't like opera and neither _____.

28

Inversion (2)
Inversion after negative adverbials

In this unit you learn to use inversion in structures that use negative adverbials to give emphasis.

Inversion occurs when broad negative adverbs or other negative adverbials are put at the beginning of a clause for emphasis. This structure is used in formal speech and writing to show something is surprising or original in some way.

Never
> Never **have I** experienced such suffering.

Barely
> Barely **had the film** ended when everyone got up to go.

Seldom
> Seldom **has hard work** been so rewarded.

Rarely
> Rarely **has so much money** been wasted by an individual.

Only once
> Only once **have I** declined their invitation.

No sooner … than
> No sooner **had I** seen the man than he disappeared.

Scarcely
> Scarcely **had he** got up when someone started hammering at the front door.

Little
> Little **did he** realize what would happen to him.

Not once
> Not once **did they** think to ask how I was.

Not in a
> Not in a thousand years **would I** agree to marry you.

> ## Remember!
> Inversion also occurs in formal speech and writing after adverbials preceded by **only**.
> *Only with exceptional luck **will you** win anything.*
> *Only when the music stopped **did Sue** finally stop dancing.*

Exercise 1

Match the sentence halves.

1 Never has there been a
2 Seldom have I encountered
3 No sooner had Carla woken
4 Rarely did a day go by
5 Not once did he think to ask
6 Scarcely had we sat down when

a he launched into a torrent of accusations.
b when I was not reminded of Larry.
c for our opinion on the matter.
d such despair in one so young.
e than she insisted on calling Max again.
f better time to invest in gold.

Exercise 2

Complete the sentences by writing one word in each gap.

| realize | express | achieve | seen | fall | entered |

1 Rarely have I _____ such a magnificent floral display.
2 Never in his life would he _____ such success again.
3 Only once did she _____ short of her own high standards of honesty.
4 Not once did he _____ any doubts about his course of action.
5 Barely had he _____ the room when Olivia started shouting wild accusations at him.
6 Little did we _____ what difficulties lay ahead of us.

Exercise 3

Put each sentence into the correct order.

1 did we suspect / had the document / all along / . / Little / that she had

_____

2 Only after / . / spot the repair / was it / careful examination / possible to

_____

3 was the problem / the armed forces / . / than within / more evident / Nowhere

_____

4 her colleagues / had she / Rarely / to this extent / . / had to rely on

_____

5 this disease / children with / . / so many / had I seen / Never before

_____

6 when chaos / Barely had / in the hall / broke out / . / the speaker finished

_____

Exercise 4

Decide if the pairs of sentences have the same meaning.

1 A Never had I been so frightened in my life.
  B I had never been so frightened before. ☐

2 A Rarely has there been a more popular prime minister.
  B Prime ministers are usually unpopular. ☐

3 A Only with a great deal of effort did we complete the work.
  B We made a great deal of effort and completed the work. ☐

4 A No sooner had I mended the chair than Michael broke it again.
  B Michael broke the chair just before I mended it again. ☐

5 A I usually dined alone in the evenings.
  B Seldom was there an evening when I dined alone. ☐

6 A I only locked up for the night after the last people had left.
  B Only when the last people had left did I lock up for the night. ☐

Exercise 5

Which sentences are correct?

1 Nowhere were the documents to be found. ☐

2 Not only I did all the shopping, but I had to cook dinner too. ☐

3 Barely the music had finished when the fighting began. ☐

4 He never did a day's work in his life, and neither did his father. ☐

5 Never there were two people less suited to parenthood. ☐

6 Little did we know what would happen next. ☐

Exercise 6

Write the missing words in sentence B so that it means the same as sentence A.

1 A I have never felt so sick in my life.

  B Never in my life _____ sick.

2 A You will only succeed with a lot of hard work.

  B Only with a lot of hard work _____.

3 A He would not hurt his mother in a million years.

  B Not in a million years _____ mother.

4 A There weren't any windows in the room either.

  B Neither _____ room.

5 A I had hardly finished my dinner when he called.

  B Hardly _____ when he called.

6 A She didn't thank us once.

  B Not once _____.

29

Inversion (3)

Inversion after *as* and *than*

In this unit you learn to use inversion in structures that compare or show similarity between two different things.

Inversion after *as*

As can be followed by an auxiliary verb (or the verb **to be**) which is inverted with the subject. The structure indicates a similarity between the two things compared in the sentence. For example, *The sitting room was found to be filthy, as **was the kitchen*** focuses on the fact that both rooms were similarly dirty.

> *Our neighbours refused to pay the money, as **did we** once we knew the plumber was overcharging.*
> *James is going to go to the local school, as **will Harry** when he's old enough.*

Inversion after *than*

Than can be followed by an auxiliary verb (or the verb **to be**) which is inverted with the subject. The structure indicates a comparison between things or people. For example, *People living in the countryside have fewer leisure opportunities than **do those** living in the city* focuses on the comparison between the two groups of people.

> *The stars of US films are often better known than **are the stars** of our own, home-grown cinema.*
> *Delegates attending my afternoon session will have a shorter lunch break than **will those** attending Mr Wilson's session.*

Exercise 1

Match the sentence halves.

1 Learning in a class is, for me, far more effective

2 A printed dictionary is nicer to use

3 Learning my third and fourth languages seemed easier

4 Tired and stressed students remember less

5 Books that have very tiny print seem harder to understand

6 Doing my shopping at the supermarket is more time-consuming

a than do those with larger type.

b than doing it online.

c than do those that are more relaxed.

d than did learning my second.

e than an online version, I think.

f than learning independently.

Exercise 2

Find the wrong or extra word in each sentence.

1 Henry always gave his children stunning birthday presents, as they did his mother and father.

2 Bus ticket prices will rise in the new year, as will rise train and underground prices.

3 Pedro and Nina have just started as going dancing on a Friday night, as have their friends Mike and Tanya.

4 The vegetables we get from Mr Tyson's shop are more fresher than those we buy anywhere else.

5 Facial expressions can communicate more feelings than can express words.

6 My sister has got a boyfriend at the University of Hong Kong, as has got my friend, Natasha.

Exercise 3

Choose the correct word.

1 The train station is usually very busy in the mornings, **as / than** is the bus station.

2 Klaus is passionate about painting, **as / than** is his father.

3 Tom followed the leader, as **was / did** the rest of the climbing group, up the south side of the peak and finally to the top.

4 The books on the tables in the centre of the shop sell much more quickly than **do / sell** those on the shelves.

5 I'd like to offer you many congratulations on your engagement, as **had / would** everyone else in my family.

6 The people who had arrived earliest got a much better view of the performance than **did / had** the rest of us.

Exercise 4

Write the correct form of the verb in brackets to complete each sentence.

1 Children who _____ (eat) healthily generally behave better in school than do those with unhealthy diets.

2 Katy _____ (have) a natural ability to run fast, as does her brother.

3 House prices in the east of the country _____ (increase), as did those in the south.

4 Johnnie had _____ (know) Jorge for ten years, as had Jim, before they set up a business together.

5 Travelling has _____ (teach) me much more than has reading thousands of books.

6 I _____ (still wait) for my results, as is everyone who took the exam on 20 May.

Exercise 5

Complete the sentences by writing one word in each gap.

1 The horse escaped through the open gate, as _____ the cows.

2 Athletes need to eat a lot more carbohydrates than _____ people who exercise little.

3 Simon thought that the hotel was superb, as _____ most people who stayed there.

4 My great aunt Janie looks more like me than _____ anyone else in my family.

5 His latest thriller will in the future be recognized as a masterpiece, as _____ his three earlier works.

6 Teri's got much more self-confidence than _____ many people of our age.

Exercise 6

Which sentences are correct?

1 Children attending the morning swimming classes will have longer sessions than will those in the afternoon. ❏

2 The names of French wines are still better known than do the wines of most other nations. ❏

3 Some of the singers at the festival were worse than were those at my five-year-old daughter's school concert! ❏

4 The ferry left on time, than did the train and the bus that I had to take to get to the meeting. ❏

5 Gerald will be pleased with the outcome of our discussion, as will Harry, I think. ❏

6 After the interview Jane was sure, as did her interviewer, that she would be the right person for the job. ❏

Exercise 7

Are the highlighted words correct or incorrect in the sentences?

1 The front door was open, **as was** ❏ the outer door.

2 After the operation, your hand will feel tight, **as will do your lower arm** ❏ .

3 Indoor plants need more light and water **than do** ❏ the same plants outdoors.

4 When asked who was responsible, Lucia remained silent, **as did** ❏ the others.

5 Doctors are better equipped to make these decisions **as are** ❏ the patients.

6 Frozen foods retain more nutrients **than do retain those** ❏ which are tinned.

Inversion (4)

Inversion after adverbials of place

In this unit you learn to use inversion in structures that add emphasis to the position or motion of the subject.

To add emphasis and drama to speech or writing it is possible to have adverbs of direction or place at the beginning of a clause, followed by a verb of motion and a noun subject. The verb and subject are inverted.

*Down the stairs **came the queen**, dressed in a silk gown.*
*Out **went the soldier**, into the dark night.*

However, if the subject is a pronoun, you put it before the verb, so there is no inversion.

*Down the stairs **she came**.*
*Out **he went**, into the dark night.*

In written English, adverb phrases introduced by prepositions such as **in the corner** can be followed by verbs indicating position, such as **crouch**, **hang**, **lie**, **stand**, etc., followed by a noun subject.

*From the ceiling **hung party decorations**.*
*In the corner **stood an old chest of drawers**.*

Again, if you use a pronoun as the subject, you put it before the verb, so there is no inversion.

*From the ceiling **they hung**.*
*In the corner **it stood**.*

You can follow **here** and **there** by the verbs **be**, **come** and **go** and a noun subject. Used at the beginning of the sentence, **here** and **there** carry more stress than they do when they come after the verb and there is usually a difference in meaning.

*Here **is the bus**.*
*There **is Jasmine**.*
*There **goes our train**.*
*Here **comes the food**.*

If the subject is a pronoun, it comes before the verb, so there is no inversion.

*Here **it comes**.*
*There **they go**.*

Exercise 1

Match the sentence halves.

1 On the seat lay
2 Down came the rain
3 Up we went in the lift
4 Out you come
5 There you are,
6 Off we went into

a a pair of red leather gloves.
b to the 25th floor.
c from your little hiding place.
d the orchard for a picnic.
e and watered the arid soil.
f I've been looking for you for ages!

Exercise 2

Choose the correct word.

1 **Down / On / In** you get, and don't forget to put your seat belt on.
2 **Off / On / Under** you go, and take your coat because it'll get cold later.
3 **Over / Out / In** they came from the stadium, waving their football scarves.
4 **Up / Down / Over** came the sun as we had breakfast on the terrace.
5 **Under / Over / Along** the shore came a lone rider on a white horse.
6 **Next / Beside / Besides** the driver sat a small boy.

Exercise 3

Find the wrong or extra word in each sentence.

1 Beside to me, my daughter was sleeping peacefully.
2 There is you are, playing computer games as usual.
3 Out you get from, and don't go in there again!
4 Down did he fell from his horse.
5 Under the floorboards beneath, we found what looked like a hand-drawn map.
6 There goes it our bus!

Exercise 4

Are the highlighted words correct or incorrect in the sentences?

1 **Beside** ☐ the lake sat an elderly woman wearing a strange hat.
2 Well, **along** ☐ you go, and have a nice day at the festival.
3 **Out** ☐ came the sun and dried up all the puddles.
4 **Where** ☐ you are? Why didn't you answer when I called?
5 **Off** ☐ you go, and don't be back late; dinner's at 7.
6 **Into** ☐ the room came a very distinguished-looking man.

Exercise 5

Which sentences are correct?

1 Off went we on our weekend camping trip. ❑

2 Out of the tree flew a beautiful multi-coloured bird. ❑

3 There are you; I thought I'd find you here! ❑

4 Get up you. Have you hurt your knee? ❑

5 Down the flag came at the end of the ceremony. ❑

6 Next to the river runs a narrow path. ❑

Exercise 6

Write the missing words in sentence B so that it means the same as sentence A.

1 **A** Oh, that's where you are.

  B Oh, there _____.

2 **A** Get up and I'll wipe the mud off your trousers.

  B Up _____ and I'll wipe the mud off your trousers.

3 **A** There's a stream that flows through the farm.

  B Through _____ a stream.

4 **A** There was a stranger standing next to my mother.

  B Next to my mother was _____.

5 **A** Go and play now.

  B Off _____ now and play.

6 **A** Come in and shut the door.

  B In _____, and shut the door.

Answer key

1 Adjectives (1)

Exercise 1

1 for
2 about
3 of
4 in
5 for
6 at

Exercise 2

1 of ✓
2 for ✗
3 over ✓
4 around ✓
5 about ✗
6 for ✓

Exercise 3

1 of
2 for
3 to
4 about
5 at
6 with

Exercise 4

1 disappointed about it.
2 good to them.
3 afraid of it.
4 glad of it.
5 responsible for it.

Exercise 5

1 f
2 d
3 a
4 e
5 c
6 b

Exercise 6

1 for ✓
2 about ✓
3 with ✗
4 with ✗
5 in ✓
6 to ✓

Exercise 7

1 but he's not very happy with it.
2 and he's very upset about it.
3 and demanded to know who was responsible for the mess.
4 and I feel really sorry for her.
5 everyone was very nice to him.

2 Adjectives (2)

Exercise 1

1 frightened faces of the children as they clung to their parents.
2 two sleeping babies.
3 similar outlooks on life.
4 burning building.
5 a solitary figure.

Exercise 2

1 living ✓
2 alive ✗
3 hurt ✗
4 injured ✓
5 happy ✓
6 glad ✗

Exercise 3

1 f
2 e
3 d
4 b
5 c
6 a

Exercise 4

1 No
2 Yes
3 Yes
4 Yes
5 Yes
6 No

Exercise 5

1 f
2 g
3 c
4 a
5 e
6 h
7 d
8 b

Exercise 6

1 worst abuse
2 highest score
3 only thing
4 last man
5 first payment
6 only software

3 Adjectives (3)

Exercise 1

1 corrected
2 empowering
3 rising
4 anticipated
5 elected
6 insinuating

Exercise 2

1 off-putting
2 absent-minded
3 able-bodied
4 thick-skinned
5 light-hearted
6 long-lost

Exercise 3

1 empty-handed
2 tongue-tied
3 death-defying
4 panic-stricken
5 long-suffering

Exercise 4

1 overgrown	4 overhanging
2 underachieving	5 underlying
3 overrated	6 understaffed

Exercise 5

1 No	3 No	5 Yes
2 Yes	4 Yes	

Exercise 6

1 The track was darkened with overhanging trees.
2 Operations were cancelled because the hospital was understaffed.
3 In my view, the band is overrated.
4 Never eat underdone meat or fish.
5 Many underdeveloped countries depend on grants.
6 The path was overgrown with grass.

Exercise 7

1 No	3 Yes	5 No
2 Yes	4 No	6 Yes

4 Adjectives and adverbs

Exercise 1

1 No	3 Yes	5 Yes
2 Yes	4 No	

Exercise 2

1 No	3 No	5 No
2 Yes	4 Yes	6 Yes

Exercise 3

1 wide	3 tight	5 close
2 rightly	4 fine	6 clearly

Exercise 4

1 tight ✓	3 wide ✗	5 freely ✓
2 right ✓	4 sharply ✗	6 fast ✓

Exercise 5

1 clean	3 sharply	5 right
2 lately	4 directly	6 overly

Exercise 6

1 sharply	3 directly	5 sharp
2 direct	4 clear	6 clearly

Exercise 7

1 because he had arrived late to school.
2 but today he's feeling fine.

3 that she could scarcely open her eyes.
4 because I would dearly love to go.
5 Lara couldn't do it right.
6 because he always worked very hard.

5 Possessive adjectives

Exercise 1

1 us	3 His	5 me
2 him	4 them	6 her

Exercise 2

1 b	3 a	5 d
2 e	4 f	6 c

Exercise 3

1 The baby's crying kept me up all night.
2 Kate heard him creeping up the stairs.
3 She doesn't mind us being here as long as we're quiet.
4 Heidi's screaming at the television was getting on my nerves.
5 Her stealing the limelight came as no great surprise.
6 I can't watch him putting in his contact lenses – urgh!

Exercise 4

1 Her having been fired lowered her self-esteem.
2 It bothered her, not being allowed to borrow his iPad.
3 She didn't mind not going away on holiday.
4 They watched us coming up the driveway but refused to open the door.
5 Ernie saw her looking at him and smiled.
6 Julio's being a pilot impressed Cindy.

Exercise 5

1 having	3 them	5 her
2 me	4 mind	6 their

6 those + participle adjectives

Exercise 1

1 worried	4 wishing
2 wanting	5 intending
3 concerned	6 affected

Exercise 2

1 All those competitors remaining in the room have passed the final test – well done!

2 The men running away from me must have been the ones who'd stolen my money.

3 I couldn't be bothered to open the book lying on my bedside table.

4 The boy playing a game on his phone looked up as I sat down next to him.

5 I approached the man sitting by the entrance door.

6 All those surprised by the result of the experiment please raise your hands.

Exercise 3

1	f	3	e	5	d
2	a	4	c	6	b

Exercise 4

1	Yes	3	No	5	Yes
2	No	4	Yes		

Exercise 5

1 Lucy is the girl lying on the sofa.

2 We were kept awake by the wind howling round the house.

3 The holiday advertised in the newspaper was a great bargain.

4 The message delivered by the boy was a complete surprise.

5 The missing cat was found lying under my desk.

6 The person teaching yoga today is fantastic.

Exercise 6

1	unfolding	4	travelling
2	giving	5	sitting
3	passed	6	judged

7 Relative clauses

Exercise 1

1	Yes	4	No
2	No	5	Yes
3	Yes	6	No

Exercise 2

1	which	4	to construct
2	who	5	Who
3	whom	6	from which

Exercise 3

1	friends	4	youngest
2	confidence	5	writer
3	girlfriends	6	house

Exercise 4

1	in	4	with
2	which	5	whom
3	to	6	over

Exercise 5

1	for whom	4	oldest of whom
2	on which	5	of which
3	with which	6	most of whom

Exercise 6

1	for ✓	4	of whom ✗
2	who ✗	5	of which ✓
3	for keeping ✗	6	of whom ✓

Exercise 7

1	whom ✓	4	which ✓
2	whom ✗	5	which ✗
3	what ✗	6	that ✗

Exercise 8

1 The book is dedicated to my parents, without whom it could not have been written.

2 The dentist gave me a special device with which to clean between my teeth.

3 The folder contains several photographs of people, on top of which is stamped the word 'traitor'.

4 Her real name is Elise, but Ellen is the name by which she prefers to be known.

5 Hoskins was the man with whom she had been living since the previous year.

6 The company pays for our hotel and food, but there is a limit above which we are not allowed to go.

8 Conditionals

Exercise 1

1	Yes	4	Yes
2	No	5	Yes
3	No		

Exercise 2

1 Were	**4** Should
2 should	**5** Were
3 Had	**6** If

Exercise 3

1 had	**5** would
2 should	**6** have
3 were	**7** did
4 are	

Exercise 4

1 should ✓	**4** Had ✗
2 did ✗	**5** known ✓
3 he ✗	**6** should ✓

Exercise 5

1 No	**4** Yes
2 Yes	**5** No
3 No	**6** Yes

Exercise 6

1 Were it	**3** be locked
2 to play	**4** I known

---

9 Ways of using as and though

Exercise 1

1 f	**4** c
2 e	**5** b
3 d	**6** a

Exercise 2

1 Yes	**3** Yes	**5** Yes
2 No	**4** No	

Exercise 3

1 for	**4** though *or* if
2 for	**5** As
3 though *or* as	**6** Much

Exercise 4

1 for	**4** to
2 if	**5** though
3 for	**6** for

Exercise 5

1 Yes	**4** Yes
2 No	**5** No
3 Yes	**6** Yes

Exercise 6

1 as she	**3** as to
2 Much	**4** for Emma

---

10 Using it as an object in sentences

Exercise 1

1 d	**4** f
2 e	**5** c
3 b	**6** a

Exercise 2

1 No	**4** Yes
2 Yes	**5** No
3 No	**6** Yes

Exercise 3

1 owe	**4** make
2 hate	**5** find
3 take	**6** love

Exercise 4

1 He made it difficult for me to refuse the job offer.

2 I found it upsetting to be dismissed by text message.

3 We all like it when we receive compliments.

4 Bob leaves it to his wife to organize their social life.

5 You owe it to yourself to work hard.

6 He sees it as insulting if people address him incorrectly.

Exercise 5

1 it	**4** as
2 as	**5** to
3 when *or* if	**6** leaves

Exercise 6

1 Lena thought it strange that there were few personal photographs.

2 made it easier to see in the thick fog.

3 I didn't mean you to take it as a criticism.

4 she saw it as a welcome interruption.

5 I thought it surprising that she already knew my name.

6 you may find it interesting to compare the two.

11 Using comparative structures for cause and effect

Exercise 1

1 f		**4** c	
2 a		**5** d	
3 e		**6** b	

Exercise 2

1 The more I learn, the less I know.

2 The darker it is, the harder it is to see.

3 The bigger the chicken, the fatter the fox.

4 The less I sleep, the more tired I become.

5 The more it rains, the likelier it is to flood.

6 The colder it is, the less I want to go out.

Exercise 3

1 No		**4** Yes	
2 Yes		**5** Yes	
3 No		**6** No	

Exercise 4

1 ore		**4** arder	
2 ess		**5** atter	
3 ealthier		**6** nnoyed *or* ngry	

Exercise 5

1 The louder they shout, the less I want to listen.

2 The more passionately they argue, the less I believe them.

3 The more time I have, the less I seem to get done.

4 The bigger my handbag, the more I find to put in it.

5 The faster I pedal, the sooner I will reach my destination.

6 The more money I make, the more I can donate to others.

Exercise 6

1 Yes	**3** Yes	**5** Yes
2 No	**4** No	**6** No

Exercise 7

1 about what you have been doing, the better.

2 the harder her heart pumped.

3 the better he felt he knew them.

4 the higher the sun protection you will need.

5 the easier it is to exercise indoors.

6 the less you will pay in tax.

12 Using -ing clauses after certain verbs

Exercise 1

1 it had us crying with laughter.

2 flowers growing in the garden.

3 cutting herself a huge slice of cheesecake.

4 living in that remote farmhouse?

5 everyone talking to each other at parties.

6 the clock working again.

Exercise 2

1 d	**3** c	**5** f
2 e	**4** a	**6** b

Exercise 3

1 going	**4** worrying
2 wearing	**5** frying
3 playing	**6** sitting

Exercise 4

1 You've got me thinking I might apply for that job.

2 Could you watch the children playing in the garden while I cook dinner?

3 I can hear the man in the flat above playing the violin every weekend.

4 Please get everyone sitting down before you make the announcement.

5 How do you find working in such a small office?

6 Can you see the bird with white tail feathers feeding by the gate?

Exercise 5

1 Yes	**3** Yes	**5** Yes
2 No	**4** No	**6** No

Exercise 6

1 Yes	**3** No	**5** Yes
2 No	**4** Yes	**6** Yes

Exercise 7

1 How does she find living out in the countryside?

2 Zoe soon had us all laughing.

3 You won't catch me wearing a bikini.

4 We could hear the wind blowing through the trees.

5 Leo noticed them talking to each other during the break.

6 Michelle could feel something brushing against her face in the darkness.

13 Focusing sentences (1)

Exercise 1
1 d
2 e
3 f
4 b
5 a
6 c

Exercise 2
1 It was Martin who won the prize.
2 It's Saturday we're going to the cinema.
3 It'll be ten years in June since we got married.
4 How can it be that this machine still doesn't work?
5 Could it have been Simon who sent the Valentine's card?
6 I don't know whether it will be in July that we move.

Exercise 3
1 it
2 wasn't
3 been
4 who
5 not
6 that's

Exercise 4
1 No
2 No
3 Yes
4 No
5 No
6 Yes

Exercise 5
1 It ✓
2 who ✗
3 that ✓
4 they're ✗
5 been ✓
6 which ✗

Exercise 6
1 Yes
2 Yes
3 No
4 No
5 No
6 Yes

14 Focusing sentences (2)

Exercise 1
1 d
2 e
3 f
4 a
5 b
6 c

Exercise 2
1 is ✓
2 did ✗
3 was ✓
4 do ✓
5 wants ✓
6 have ✗

Exercise 3
1 What happens is, you fill out the application form and they contact you by email.
2 What you do is your own business.
3 What I tend to do is smile, nod and pretend I understand.
4 What works is holding your nose and counting to 20.
5 What I couldn't understand was why they hadn't phoned.
6 What surprises me most is that she's achieved so much and yet she's still only 21.

Exercise 4
1 What
2 What he bought was
3 What she does is
4 What is lacking
5 he will do is
6 What I tried was adding

Exercise 5
1 is
2 was
3 did
4 had
5 didn't
6 What

15 Using to-infinitive clauses as subject/object

Exercise 1
1 b
2 e
3 a
4 f
5 c
6 d

Exercise 2
1 Yes
2 Yes
3 No
4 No

Exercise 3
1 to drink
2 are
3 to stay
4 was
5 to talk
6 didn't know *or* did not know

Exercise 4
1 To see dolphins in their natural environment was magical.
2 The text to read for homework is on page 45.

3 The hospital needs two nurses to look after sick children.

    4 Stefan doesn't like anyone to sit in his seat.

    5 To win so much money would make anyone happy.

    6 Something tasty to eat was what he wanted most at this moment.

Exercise 5

1 to wear.   **4** was difficult to find.

2 is madness!   **5** must be great.

3 to watch.

Exercise 6

1 the first girl at our school to win a scholarship.

2 any chance to play sport.

3 but Rita was the only one to go to university.

4 we haven't found a house to move into yet.

5 to learn new skills.

6 like anything to drink?

Exercise 7

1 Yes   **3** No   **5** No

2 Yes   **4** No   **6** Yes

Exercise 8

1 to consider   **4** save

2 to save   **5** to do

3 consider   **6** to help

16 Using negatives with reporting verbs

Exercise 1

1 a   **3** e   **5** b

2 d   **4** f   **6** c

Exercise 2

1 she even needs to work

2 she will

3 she is

4 she does

5 she ever diets

6 she even knows who I am

Exercise 3

1 I predict he won't win the election.

2 I bet he won't even remember me.

3 I assume you haven't heard the news.

4 I sincerely hope the market doesn't crash.

5 I presume they haven't left yet.

6 I suspect they don't have much money.

Exercise 4

1 No   **4** Yes

2 No   **5** Yes

3 Yes   **6** No

Exercise 5

1 suppose   **4** imagine

2 think   **5** believe

3 expect

Exercise 6

1 she won't want to go

2 he'll be more than 30 *or* he can be more then 30

3 Clare's spoken to her manager

4 they won't visit us again

17 Passives (1)

Exercise 1

1 were shown the letter

2 were fed the leftovers

3 were given to his wife

4 was awarded several prizes

5 was bought everything

6 were allocated half an hour

Exercise 2

1 be awarded   **4** were shown

2 was announced **5** was found

3 had been given **6** is paid

Exercise 3

1 it was proved to his employer

2 will be paid to all staff

3 the safety measures were explained to them

4 All his children

5 were sent to

6 The findings were reported to us

Exercise 4

1 We were allocated an office at the back of the building.

2 It was explained to us that the tickets were not refundable.

3 It was announced to the audience that the lead actor was sick.

4 She was sent a letter by the school to tell her that her daughter had been excluded.

5 The journalists were given special passes to allow them into the conference hall.

6 The charity has been awarded a grant to extend its services over a wider area.

Exercise 5

1 awarded
2 demonstrated
3 played
4 poured
5 reported
6 fed

Exercise 6

1 To me was guaranteed ✗
2 to the prime minister ✓
3 To all staff ✗
4 were not told ✓
5 was refused entry ✓
6 was lent the princess ✗

Exercise 7

1 Yes
2 No
3 Yes
4 No
5 Yes
6 No

Exercise 8

1 Yes
2 No
3 No
4 No
5 Yes
6 Yes

Exercise 9

1 will be presented to the winning gymnast at the end of the tournament.

2 he is only fed the finest beef steak.

3 are taught on the course.

4 will be sent home to your parents.

5 the need for secrecy was emphasized to all staff.

6 it had been given to her by Ben.

18 Passives (2)

Exercise 1

1 b
2 a
3 d
4 c
5 e

Exercise 2

1 being
2 to be
3 being
4 to be
5 to be
6 to be

Exercise 3

1 served
2 being
3 said
4 told
5 mind

Exercise 4

1 Yes
2 No
3 Yes
4 Yes
5 No

Exercise 5

1 Yes
2 No
3 No
4 Yes
5 No
6 No

Exercise 6

1 The bones are thought to be from a meat-eating dinosaur.

2 He put a helmet on because he didn't want to be hit by a falling rock.

3 I didn't mean what I said to be taken seriously.

4 Being chosen to play in the match was a big surprise.

5 Does your son remember being put to bed last night?

6 Putting the lid on the pan prevents the rice drying out.

Exercise 7

1 is said to have been named after Christopher Columbus.

2 being spoken to like a naughty child.

3 something has to be done soon.

4 after having been rescued by emergency services.

5 to be known as Bella.

6 he noticed that he was being followed.

19 Future perfect

Exercise 1

1 have gone
2 get
3 have done
4 have met
5 tell

Exercise 2

1 Katya won't have arrived yet, will she?

2 They won't have had time to clean the house properly yet.

3 Helen will change her mind by tomorrow.

4 My grandparents will have been married for 60 years next August.

5 Lucia won't have been told about Chris's promotion yet, I presume.

6 How many runners will have finished by midday?

Exercise 3

1 by

2 married

3 before

4 been

5 realized

6 seen

Exercise 4

1 teaching ✓

2 studied ✗

3 starts ✓

4 won't have ✓

5 will have done ✓

6 have you finished ✗

Exercise 5

1 The train will have left by the time we get to the station.

2 I'm going into town on Saturday, but the jeans I want will probably have sold out by then.

3 When the Smiths leave tomorrow evening, we'll have had a whole weekend of their complaining!

4 The restaurant will close before we get there if you don't hurry up.

5 Don't worry, that noise will only have been my brother's motorbike.

6 The rain is forecast to carry on until Tuesday, by which time it will have caused the river to overflow its banks.

Exercise 6

1 have started

2 gone to sleep

3 left

4 run out

5 writing

6 don't think

20 Should and the subjunctive

Exercise 1

1 get

2 train

3 asked

4 should

5 join

6 pay

Exercise 2

1 No

2 Yes

3 Yes

4 No

5 Yes

Exercise 3

1 c

2 d

3 e

4 b

5 a

Exercise 4

1 worn

2 is

3 take

4 leave

5 accompany

6 was

Exercise 5

1 Who on earth suggested the canteen be painted bright purple?

2 It is vital that everyone should understand the safety procedure.

3 It's not essential that *all* employees approve the new design, as long as most do!

4 My friends recommended that we should eat in the Greengate Café.

5 Can I just ask that the cat be well looked after while we're away?

6 It is vital that Tilly see the doctor as soon as possible.

21 Avoiding repetition by omitting to- infinitives

Exercise 1

1 f

2 c

3 e

4 a

5 b

6 d

Exercise 2

1 failed

2 manage

3 struggle

4 hesitate

5 decide

6 mean

Exercise 3

1 deserve

2 mean

3 expected

4 afford

5 requested

6 appeared

Exercise 4

1 I intended to email him but forgot.

2 I'll come out tonight if I'm allowed to.

3 He can join us for dinner tonight if he chooses to.

4 I'd leave my job if I dared to.

5 We could sell the house if we had to.

6 You can pay now if you wish to.

Exercise 5

1 No   3 Yes   5 Yes

2 No   4 Yes   6 Yes

Exercise 6

1 if she doesn't want to.

2 if he tries.

3 if you like.

4 but he didn't intend to.

5 as I had told them to be.

6 because she was expected to.

Exercise 7

1 Yes   3 Yes   5 Yes

2 No   4 No   6 Yes

22 Politeness

Exercise 1

1 f   3 e   5 d

2 a   4 c   6 b

Exercise 2

1 I was hoping to borrow your car tonight.

2 What kind of jacket were you looking for?

3 Was there an author you particularly liked?

4 We were wondering if you could give us a donation?

5 I wanted to ask if the heating could be turned down.

6 Excuse me, did you want something?

Exercise 3

1 wondering   4 hoping

2 might   5 hoped

3 Was

Exercise 4

1 wondering   3 looking

2 Would   4 hoping

Exercise 5

1 Yes   4 No

2 No   5 Yes

3 Yes

Exercise 6

1 No   4 No

2 No   5 Yes

3 Yes   6 Yes

Exercise 7

1 wondering   3 ask   5 if

2 were   4 it   6 there

23 Sentence connectors and conjunctions

Exercise 1

1 Consequently ✓   4 Furthermore ✗

2 However ✓   5 Furthermore ✓

3 Hence ✓   6 Therefore ✓

Exercise 2

1 therefore   4 however

2 meanwhile   5 by contrast

3 whereas   6 nevertheless

Exercise 3

1 my sister has 23.

2 we were perfectly content with our lives.

3 we had each other.

4 I was living on a meagre diet of bread and water.

5 we recommend that you apply for housing before the official deadline.

Exercise 4

1 Yes   3 Yes

2 Yes   4 No

Exercise 5

1 Yes   3 Yes   5 Yes

2 Yes   4 No   6 No

Exercise 6

1 Meanwhile   4 Furthermore

2 However   5 Nevertheless

3 Consequently

24 Which, whose, how much *and* how many

Exercise 1

1 d   3 c   5 f

2 e   4 b   6 a

Exercise 2

1 do you consider it

2 do you think is used

3 will you ask

4 are you planning

5 do researchers often find

6 was the questionnaire

Exercise 3

1	Yes	**3**	No	**5**	No
2	No	**4**	Yes	**6**	Yes

Exercise 4

1 should children under the age of 14 be accompanied by ✓

2 you said offered to help us ✗

3 should we not disturb ✓

4 did you go where had you never been ✗

5 did John offer to help us by doing ✓

6 car manufacturer has just withdrawn their latest model ✓

Exercise 5

1 How large a percentage of people who buy this brand of washing powder are in the top three socio-economic classes?

2 Which station did you say I should get off at?

3 How much more did Mario spend during his holiday than he intended?

4 Who do you think Stefan saw crossing the road outside the supermarket?

5 How long did he say he was going to wait for?

6 What do you think we should ask Daphne to bring to the meeting?

Exercise 6

1	No	**3**	No	**5**	Yes
2	Yes	**4**	Yes	**6**	No

Exercise 7

1 which sort of tree trapped the most air pollution.

2 whose daughter he had taken to the cinema.

3 did you make a cover for?

4 did you put in the pies?

5 whose essay Michel had copied his from.

6 do staff spend speaking on the phone?

25 Phrasal verbs (1)

Exercise 1

1 switched on my computer ✓

2 for me to take in ✓

3 The course goes on ✓

4 picking them up ✗

5 hand in ✗

6 hang us out ✗

Exercise 2

1 down.

2 up my earring?, it up?

3 up all the things I do that get me down.

4 on.

5 for a new bike.

Exercise 3

1 Can you come and pick me up from Lara's?

2 Please try not to wake us up.

3 Jacob's looking for his phone in the café.

4 You mustn't give in to temptation!

5 Have you found out when Rick is coming to stay?

6 I've never before come across this type of dance music.

Exercise 4

1	at, for	**3**	after, for
2	him, it	**4**	back it, out it

Exercise 5

1 The concert organizers have decided to put it off until the singer has recovered.

2 Please go away until I've finished my work.

3 I hope they never find out who made the mistake.

4 My grandparents brought me and my brothers up.

5 I know I can always count on Tom.

6 She filled in the form very quickly.

Exercise 6

1	e	**3**	b	**5**	d
2	c	**4**	f	**6**	a

26 Phrasal verbs (2)

Exercise 1

1 it down to

2 looking forward to a break

3 it up with her

4 out for students

5 up for what he believed in

Exercise 2

1 back
2 up
3 him
4 college
5 his stuff
6 me

Exercise 3

1 away with it
2 up on your news
3 him out of
4 get on with her
5 you up to
6 run out of them

Exercise 4

1 I need to cut down on the amount of money I spend.
2 Be off with you!
3 She wrapped the broken vase up in newspaper and threw it away.
4 Get on with it!
5 When do you set off for work?
6 He gets annoyed if you don't go along with his wishes.

Exercise 5

1 No
2 Yes
3 No
4 No
5 Yes

Exercise 6

1 No
2 No
3 Yes
4 Yes
5 No
6 Yes

27 Inversion (1)

Exercise 1

1 was Eva
2 were so great
3 was the palace
4 is my phone
5 was her dismay
6 is such a liar

Exercise 2

1 b
2 f
3 d
4 c
5 a
6 e

Exercise 3

1 arrogance
2 miserable
3 restrictions
4 overwhelming
5 difficulty
6 admired

Exercise 4

1 Yes
2 No
3 No
4 No
5 Yes
6 Yes

Exercise 5

1 I couldn't afford the bus fare and neither could Amy.
2 So delicious were the cakes that I ate far more than I should have done.
3 Such was the force of his anger that we were quite frightened.
4 The bank isn't open today and neither is the post office.
5 Such were the dangers faced by these soldiers that many of them never recovered.
6 So outrageous did his behaviour become that even his family grew tired of him.

Exercise 6

1 high was the mountain
2 did Jan
3 was our
4 does physics
5 expensive was the restaurant
6 does my father

28 Inversion (2)

Exercise 1

1 f
2 d
3 e
4 b
5 c
6 a

Exercise 2

1 seen
2 achieve
3 fall
4 express
5 entered
6 realize

Exercise 3

1 Little did we suspect that she had had the document all along.
2 Only after careful examination was it possible to spot the repair.
3 Nowhere was the problem more evident than within the armed forces.
4 Rarely had she had to rely on her colleagues to this extent.
5 Never before had I seen so many children with this disease.
6 Barely had the speaker finished when chaos broke out in the hall.

Exercise 4

1	Yes	**3**	Yes	**5**	No
2	No	**4**	No	**6**	Yes

Exercise 5

1	Yes	**3**	No	**5**	No
2	No	**4**	Yes	**6**	Yes

Exercise 6

1 have I felt so

2 will you succeed

3 would he hurt his

4 were there any windows in the

5 had I finished my dinner

6 did she thank us

Exercise 5

1	did	**3**	did	**5**	will
2	do	**4**	does	**6**	have

Exercise 6

1	Yes	**3**	Yes	**5**	Yes
2	No	**4**	No	**6**	No

Exercise 7

1 as was ✓

2 as will do your lower arm ✗

3 than do ✓

4 as did ✓

5 as are ✗

6 than do retain those ✗

29 Inversion (3)

Exercise 1

1	f	**3**	d	**5**	a
2	e	**4**	c	**6**	b

Exercise 2

1 Henry always gave his children stunning birthday presents, as did his mother and father.

2 Bus ticket prices will rise in the new year, as will train and underground prices.

3 Pedro and Nina have just started going dancing on a Friday night, as have their friends Mike and Tanya.

4 The vegetables we get from Mr Tyson's shop are fresher than those we buy anywhere else.

5 Facial expressions can communicate more feelings than can words.

6 My sister has got a boyfriend at the University of Hong Kong, as has my friend, Natasha.

Exercise 3

1	as	**3**	did	**5**	would
2	as	**4**	do	**6**	did

Exercise 4

1 eat

2 has

3 increased

4 known

5 taught

6 'm still waiting *or* am still waiting

30 Inversion (4)

Exercise 1

1	a	**3**	b	**5**	f
2	e	**4**	c	**6**	d

Exercise 2

1	In	**3**	Out	**5**	Along
2	Off	**4**	Up	**6**	Beside

Exercise 3

1 Beside me, my daughter was sleeping peacefully.

2 There you are, playing computer games as usual.

3 Out you get, and don't go in there again!

4 Down he fell from his horse.

5 Under the floorboards, we found what looked like a hand-drawn map.

6 There goes our bus!

Exercise 4

1	Beside ✓	**3**	Out ✓	**5**	Off ✓
2	along ✗	**4**	Where ✗	**6**	Into ✓

Exercise 5

1	No	**3**	No	**5**	No
2	Yes	**4**	No	**6**	Yes

Exercise 6

1	you are	**4**	standing a stranger
2	you get	**5**	you go
3	the farm flows	**6**	you come

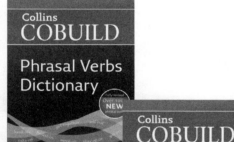